Let's THINK about Feelings
Tools for Child-Friendly Cognitive Behavioral Therapy

by
Marcie Yeager, LCSW, RPT-S
and
Daniel Yeager, LCSW, RPT-S

Golden Path Games

playtherapy@att.net

Let's THINK about Feelings

by
Marcie Yeager, LCSW, RPT-S
and
Daniel Yeager, LCSW, RPT-S

ABOUT THIS RESOURCE

This resource provides child-friendly "tools" for therapists who have previous training and expertise in cognitive-behavioral therapy. This resource is not intended to provide background or training in CBT. It is expected that therapists using this resource already have a sound theoretical understanding of CBT and a repertoire of CBT interventions that they use with clients. This resource is intended to supplement those interventions, by providing activities and visual tools that make the principles of CBT more accessible for young people.

Copying and distributing pages

Permission to copy and distribute pages from this book is granted only to the individual purchaser and only for their personal, professional and private use. Please request specific permission (playtherapy@att.net) for any other use of these materials.

This resource is also available as a digital download (with full-color, printable pages) from www.playtherapyworks.com.
See last page for more details.

© 2016 Golden Path Games
ISBN-13: 978-0692641552
ISBN-10: 0692641556

Welcome!

Ready to get started?

As you work with the activities in this book, we encourage your questions and feedback. You can reach us at playtherapy@att.net.

Overview of *Let's THINK About Feelings*

Part I:
Tools to help children differentiate emotions and identify stressors

1. Let's Talk About Feelings
This activity uses the ***Feelings Word Finder*** and the ***Here's What Happened*** cards to help children to accurately differentiate and name a wide range of emotions. The *Word Finder* has words to describe 60 emotions; the cards describe situations involving children, teens and adults.
With this activity, the child imagines how these other people might feel.
… Page 5

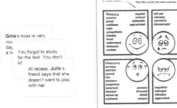

2. Feelings Check-Up
With these activities, the ***Feelings Word Finder*** is used (without the ***Here's What Happened*** cards) to help children and families identify and appropriately express their feelings about events that have occurred in their lives.
… Page 13

3. Show Me How You Feel
The ***Feeling Word Finder**-Junior version* is a simplified and more visual version of the *Word Finder*, designed especially for younger children. It features a simplified list of words in the four categories (happy, sad, mad, worried/scared) and uses pictures of faces to help children to identify the intensity of those feelings. It has its own set of ***Here's What Happened*** cards.
As with the regular *Feelings Word Finder*, it can also be used to help young children identify and appropriately express their own emotions.
… Page 16

4. Be a Feelings Detective
An important component of CBT is learning to challenge thoughts and beliefs that are inaccurate. This activity is a home assignment that begins the process of helping clients to distinguish between the "facts" of what happened and one's consequent thoughts or beliefs.
… Page 20

5. The Stressometer
The ***Stressometer*** can be used to help the client think about the difference between healthy and unhealthy stress. First, the client identifies stressors (challenges, situations, circumstances, habits, relationships) in their lives. Using the stressometer as a visual guide, the client then assesses where each of the stressors fall on the healthy-unhealthy stress continuum.
… Page 24

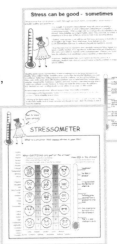

6. TOP 4 Stress Busters
This handout is a follow-up to the Stressometer activity. It sets the stage for the therapeutic interventions in the next section of this manual: *Tools to help children understand and regulate emotions and behavior*
… Page 28

1. Don't Do It!

This activity focuses on *response inhibition.* It can be difficult to apply the principles of CBT in everyday life because we may habitually respond to a given situation with an ingrained, automatic response that is not helpful. In order to practice using new thoughts, we have to first be aware of, and then inhibit, this automatic response. *Don't Do It* includes games that introduce children to the concept of response inhibition and a home assignment to connect the concept to their everyday lives.
   … Page 31

2. *Are You a Careful Thinker?*

This group of activities focuses on *cognitive flexibility.*

The *I Can Choose* activity introduces the concept of cognitive flexibility, a basic principle of CBT. The goal is to help children understand that, by changing the way that they perceive or think about situations, they can transform their emotional reactions, which in turn helps them choose the most optimal behavior.
   … Page 37

Be a Mastermind is a home assignment that helps children to stop and sort through their reactions when upsetting events occur.
… Page 43

Are You a Careful Thinker? (Junior version)
This story explains the concept of cognitive flexibility in a way that is accessible for very young children.
… Page 47

Encouraging Words
These postcards are a "take-home" follow up to the *Are You a Careful Thinker?* activities. To help the child prepare for an upcoming stressful or challenging situation, the therapist helps the child formulate "encouraging words" - short, positive statements that they can use to replace automatic anxious, angry and/or upsetting thoughts.
… Page 50

3. Slow Down and Get Calm

This activity focuses on *self-calming and self-monitoring.* In addition to inhibiting one's automatic and unhelpful thoughts in a stressful situation, it is also important to be aware of one's physiological responses and to take action to "calm down" once automatic responses are triggered. This activity teaches child-friendly techniques for self-calming. The ability to *self-monitor* one's arousal is an important skill in CBT, so this activity also includes a rating scale that can be given to the child as an aid to self-monitoring in everyday life.
… Page 53

4. What's The Problem, What's The Plan?

These activities focus on *cognitive flexibility and problem solving. What's The Problem, What's The Plan?* is designed for use with families. (There is also a version for use in individual therapy.) This activity structures the problem-solving process and also provides the child and family with a written summary of their decision-making to take home as a guide and reminder.
… Page 57

Stay-on-Track Map

A follow up to *What's The Problem, What's The Plan?,* This home assignment provides external support to help children better regulate their emotions and behavior in order to do their part in carrying out a plan.
… Page 61

Part I:

Tools to help children differentiate emotions and identify stressors

LET'S TALK ABOUT FEELINGS

Rationale: Most people are pretty good at naming the basic emotions: *happy*, *sad*, *angry*, and *scared*. But our emotions are much more complex than that! The *Feelings Word Finder* is a hands-on tool that helps children to more accurately identify feelings that they, and others, experience.

Application/Treatment modality: Individual, family, group

Goals:

With this activity, children:

- recognize the connection between situations and consequent emotions.
- identify (and discriminate between) a wide variety of emotions.
- develop insight by discussing situations faced by children, adolescents and adults.
- learn that some situations may give rise to "mixed emotions" of varying intensity.

Materials Needed:

1. *Feelings Word Finder* (page 6)

The *Word Finder* has words that can be used to describe feelings. The words are grouped into four categories: The top left section has words that describe pleasurable feelings about a situation; the top right section has words associated with sadness or regret; the lower right section has words that express dissatisfaction with a situation; the lower left section has words associated with feelings of uncertainty. (Laminate the chart for durability.)

2. *Here's What Happened* cards (pages 7-10)

Each card presents a person confronting a situation that might evoke a mixture of emotions. The persons presented include adults, teens, and children. This mixture allows players to put themselves in the place of other people, which helps players understand multiple viewpoints and aids in the development of empathy.

You can also use the blank cards on (page 11) to create your own situations.

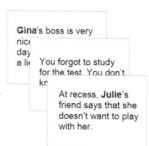

> NOTE: The cards tell only "what happened' (observable behavior) and not consequent thoughts, emotions or behavior. An important component of CBT is learning to distinguish between the facts of "what happened," the consequent thoughts and beliefs, and the impact of those cognitions on emotions and behavior. The cards help to set a foundation for making the distinction.

3. Paper clips or other small objects

Large-size paper clips can be used to mark various feeling words on the *Word Finder*. You can use plain paper clips or colored. Alternatively, any small object (such as coins or chips) can be used to mark the words.

Instructions

1. Place the *Here's What Happened* cards and the paper clips near the *Feelings Word Finder*.

2. When it is your turn, choose the top card and read it aloud. Imagine how the person described in the situation might feel. Next, using both the paper clips and the words on the board, show how you think the person might feel, by placing the paper clips on the words you choose. You can stack extra paper clips on some words to show that those are the strongest feelings. If the word you want to use isn't on the board, just name the word and then put the paper clip(s) on the *face* in that section.

> **Gina**'s boss is very nice...
> day...
> a li...
>
> You forgot to study for the test. You don't kn...
>
> At recess, **Julie**'s friend says that she doesn't want to play with her.

3. Before your turn is over, take a second look. This is especially important if all of your paper clips are in one section. Look at other sections of the board to see if there are any other emotions the person might experience in this situation.

> *Important!* There are no right or wrong answers. Another person might have very different ideas from yours. That's OK. The purpose of this activity is to get participants thinking and talking about feelings. One person might think differently about the situation and therefore have differing feelings. All discussion is encouraged!

4. After any discussion is complete, the next person takes a turn.

WHAT'S the FEELING ?

Be a feelings detective: Find the best word to express the emotion.
Remember that people may have "mixed emotions."

Add new words in the blank spaces.

Happy
pleased
proud
confident
calm
sympathetic
friendly
loved
understood
fortunate
excited

hopeful
content
optimistic
appreciated

Sad
left out
unhappy
sorrowful
discouraged

blue
lonely
guilty
ashamed
embarrassed
remorseful
disappointed
hopeless
depressed
miserable

Unsure
nervous
worried
scared
shy
insecure
suspicious
surprised
shocked
mixed-up
confused

anxious
stressed
afraid
uneasy

Mad
annoyed
disapproving
fed-up
jealous
determined
defiant
disgusted
frustrated
angry
furious

impatient
outraged
offended
aggravated

How to make the HERE'S WHAT HAPPENED cards:
1. Copy this page (card fronts).
2. If desired, on the reverse side of these cards, you can copy the "Here's What Happened" card backs (page 12)
3. Cut along the dotted lines to make cards.

Isaac still sucks his thumb at night. After his dad calls him a baby, Isaac's sister gives Isaac a hug.

Zack's new stepfather spanks him whenever he breaks a rule. Zack's mother doesn't like it, but she doesn't do anything about it.

Claire and her mom plan a party. They buy games and prizes and food and invite seven people. On the day of the party, two kids come.

Pat has a hard time sitting still. His teachers complain about this. His dad tells Pat that he was the same way when he was a boy.

Allie likes to sleep with her mother. Her mother says that it's time for her to start sleeping in her own room.

Every day, **Jake** gets picked on by the older kids at the bus stop. He has tried to get them to stop but nothing has worked.

Marisa's mom works at two jobs. After school, Marisa cleans the house and takes care of her two brothers.

At recess, **Julie**'s friend says that she doesn't want to play with her.

Eva's parents read her diary and find out what she has been doing after school. Now Eva's grandmother comes and stays with her.

Martha's friend Joe is a lot of fun to be with. But he also has a bad temper and sometimes he hurts her. Her other friends want her to stop being friends with him.

Colin's grandparents tell him that he should be more like his sister. But his mom speaks up and says that Colin is just great the way he is.

Mark is busy all the time with work. He makes lots of money but he doesn't have much time to spend with his wife and children.

Millie's son throws a tantrum when she tells him to clean his room. He tells her that he hates her.

Anna works full time and goes to school at night. Her son stays with his grandparents most of the time.

Joni has the day off and she invites her son to go to a movie. But he says he would rather play on the computer.

How to make the HERE'S WHAT HAPPENED cards:
1. Copy this page (card fronts).
2. If desired, on the reverse side of these cards, you can copy the "Here's What Happened" card backs (page 12)
3. Cut along the dotted lines to make cards.

Maria got the *Teacher of the Year* award at her school. She hears some other teachers say that she doesn't deserve it.

Max just got back from a visit with his father and stepmother. His mother asks him lots of questions about what happens at his father's house.

Al's father died three years ago. Now his mother has started to date a friend of hers. She is spending more time with the friend and less time at home with Al.

Sam's father moved away when Sam was a baby and never visited. Now Sam's father and his new wife want to start seeing Sam.

Abra's mom is finally taking her to the mall to shop for new clothes. But at the last minute, her mom has to work. So Abra's dad says that he will take her.

Mel is working hard on a science project and is almost finished. Mel's friend comes over and says, "That looks like something my baby brother would do."

Keli had a bad day at school. When she gets home her mom is very busy taking care of the baby, talking on the phone and fixing dinner.

Lyle lost his job at the factory. He stays home and takes care of the new baby.

Carla gets a call from her son's teacher. He has been fighting with the other kids at school. The teacher asks Carla to come in for a meeting.

Gina's boss is very nice to her. But one day he asks her to tell a lie for him.

Ben is invited to go on a weekend trip with a new friend. Ben's mom says he cannot go because she has never met the parents.

Jena wears a hearing aid. On the school bus, some children point to her hearing aid and whisper to one another.

Juan asks his dad for help with his science project. His dad says that he is old enough now to do it on his own.

Kyla thinks her stepmother is unfair. She talks to her dad and he tells her that she is exaggerating.

Will has a temper tantrum. His dad puts him in his room. After Will calms down, his dad comes in and talks with him about what happened.

HERE'S WHAT HAPPENED cards

How to make the HERE'S WHAT HAPPENED cards:
1. Copy this page (card fronts).
2. If desired, on the reverse side of these cards, you can copy the "Here's What Happened" card backs (page 12)
3. Cut along the dotted lines to make cards.

Nora gets into a fight with her brother. They both say mean things. After they cool down, her brother apologizes.

Zack's father played sports in high school and wants Zack to do the same. But Zack would rather spend his time playing music.

Mia has been thinking about a promise that she made. She realizes that she should never have made the promise. She decides to ask her mom what to do.

Mike takes some money from a neighbor's house. The neighbor calls Mike's mom and tells her. Mike's mom yells at the neighbor. She says Mike would never steal.

Todd's parents always tell people how smart and talented he is. Todd's brother is mean to him because Todd gets all the attention.

Ray doesn't understand math. Some of the kids say he is dumb. But his teacher tells him not to worry and gives him extra help.

Rob's friends want him to do something wrong. When he won't do it, they make fun of him. But his sister overhears and tells him he did the right thing.

Keisha wants to apply for a great new job. Her friends tell her she'll never get it, she should not even try. She applies for the job anyway.

Corey's parents say that he takes too long to get ready in the morning. So now Corey has to go to bed an hour earlier.

Manny went to the parking lot and his new car had a big dent in it. A lady says that she saw a car run into his. She wrote down the license number.

Margo's dad has to work out of town a lot. When he does, she and her sister stay at their aunt's house.

Doug is the slowest runner on his baseball team. The coach says Doug has a good arm and will make a great pitcher.

Rosa's daughter is getting a divorce. The daughter asks Rosa if she and the children can come and live with Rosa for a while.

Willa is invited to a big party. She is told not to tell her best friend, who's not invited.

Essie's new friend invites him to a party. Essie's mom finds out there will be no adults at the party. She tells him that he can't go.

How to make the HERE'S WHAT HAPPENED cards:
1. Copy this page (card fronts).
2. If desired, on the reverse side of these cards, you can copy the "Here's What Happened" card backs (page 12)
3. Cut along the dotted lines to make cards.

Toby tries out for the basketball team but doesn't make it. His coach tells him that he can try out again next year.	**Leo** is caught cheating on a test. His teacher says that he won't be punished this time if he talks with the counselor.	**Dylan** knows the answers to all the questions on the test. But he's not finished and the teacher says the time is up.
Nell is walking home. Some kids she doesn't know are playing ball in a neighbor's yard. They ask if she wants to play.	**Jude**'s parents say the clothes that he likes cost too much. So he decides to earn the money by mowing lawns.	**Julia**'s parents insist that she must always "have the best" and always "be the best."
Matt's parents are divorced. His mom lives far away. His mom calls and says she wants Matt to fly out to her house for a vacation.	**Pierre** is on the baseball team. He's not one of the good players, and he strikes out a lot. But he has made a lot of new friends on the team.	**Dan** wants to ask Tina out. He tries to talk to her, but he doesn't know what to say. She smiles at him.
Kyle's older brother bosses him around. If Kyle doesn't do what he wants, his brother threatens him.	**Tina** wants to play with her older brother. His friends tell her to go away and leave them alone. Her brother promises he will play with her later.	**Lulu**'s father has been transferred to another city. She will have be moving and living in a new house and going to a new school.
Carl signed up to play soccer, but now he wants to quit. His dad says that he has to finish the season.	**Molly** is shy about talking in front of people. Her teacher suggests she try out for the school play.	**Ezra** has a big test today. He studied hard last night. He wants to make an A.

Make your own *HERE'S WHAT HAPPENED* cards

How to make the HERE'S WHAT HAPPENED cards:
1. Write your own situations in the sections below.
2. If desired, on the reverse side of these cards, you can copy the "Here's What Happened" card backs (page 12)
3. Cut along the dotted lines to make cards.

Card Backs

1. If you want to have a back on your cards, copy this page on the reverse side of the *Here's What Happened* cards on pages 7-11.

2. Use the dotted guide lines on the card fronts to cut the cards.

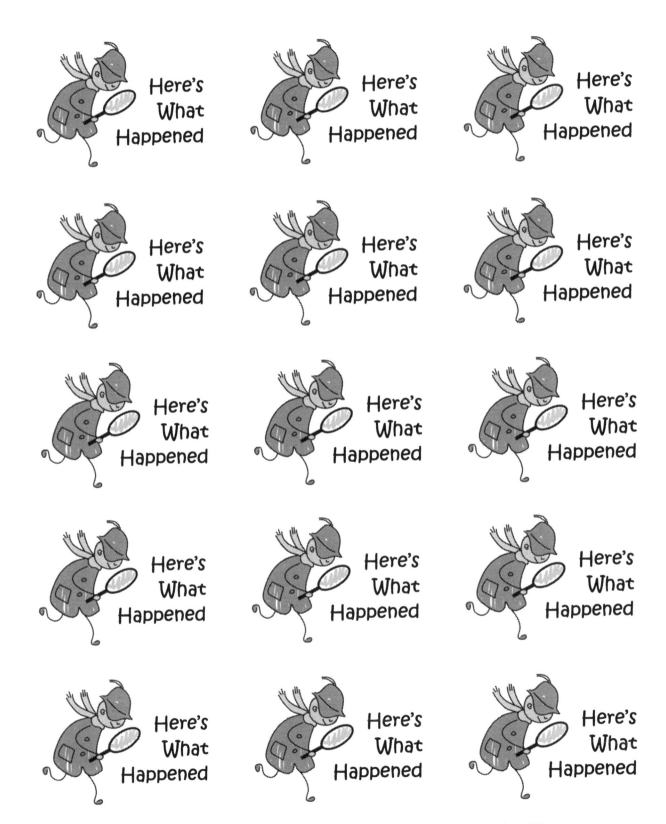

FEELINGS CHECK-UP

Rationale:

Typically a CBT session begins with a review of what has transpired since the client's last session. This activity provides a quick and easy format to help children recall events that have occurred between sessions and to more easily identify the emotions that accompanied those events.

Application/Treatment modality: Individual therapy

Goals:

With this activity, information can be gathered that helps the therapist to:
- assess the child's progress in applying CBT skills in real-life situations.
- incorporate real-life issues into whatever therapeutic interventions are planned for that session.

Materials Needed:

1) *Feelings Word Finder* (page 15)
2) Colored markers, pencils or crayons

1. Give the client a copy of the *Feelings Word Finder*. Have the client choose four colored markers, one color for each section. Ask the client to think about the some of the emotions that she or he experienced during past week (or since the last session). Then have the client underline those emotions that they experienced a little bit and circle those that they experienced a lot.

2. After this is completed, look over the list and ask the client to tell you what situation gave rise to each of those emotions, beginning with those that were experienced "a little bit." This enables the therapist to quickly gather information about:
   a) recent events that have occurred in the client's life and
   b) the client's reactions to those events.

3. The information gathered during the Check-Up can be incorporated into interventions during the session.

> Note: In addition to be using it as a quick check-up at the beginning of the therapy session, the *Feelings Word Finder* can be used at any time during a therapy session, to give children a hands-on tool to "show" how they are feeling at the moment and/or how they feel in situations that are being discussed.

A. Family Feelings Check-Up

In addition to its use in individual therapy, the *Feelings Check-Up* is a helpful tool in family therapy:

1. As a routine check-up:

- Each person can have their own copy of the chart, or they can all use the same chart and color code their responses using colored paper clips or colored pencils/markers.
- Ask each family member to think of three feelings that he or she has had in the last week (or since the last session). • Using the *Feelings Word Finder,* have each person mark those three feelings.
- Once everyone has finished, have family members take turns telling when and where they experienced each feeling. Have the first person tell one feeling, then go on to the next person.
- Continue until each person has shared all three feelings.

> Note: The therapist can ask questions for clarification. During that day's session, the therapist may want to draw on information shared through the check-in activity.

(Continued on next page)

Feelings Check-Up Instructions - Continued

2. As a way to begin processing a significant event:

During any therapy session in which the family needs to talk about a significant event, the *Feelings Check-Up* can get the ball rolling.

• Give each person a copy of the *Feelings Word Finder*.

• Have them--without speaking--mark as many feelings related to the event as are relevant to them.

• Next, give each person a turn to talk about their perceptions and thoughts about what happened.

> Note:The therapist may ask questions to clarify, but shouldn't allow in-depth discussion during this activity, as the purpose is for each person to be heard as the others listen. (However, **"active listening" skills*** can be modeled by the therapist and practiced by the family members.)

• The therapist then uses the information learned during this activity to design appropriate interventions for the therapy session.)

> ***Active Listening:** After the *speaker* describes the emotions that they felt during and after the event, the *listener* (either the therapist or one of the family members) summarizes what the speaker says. The speaker either confirms that the listener's summary is correct or, if not, clarifies what was said (in which case the listener then summarizes again.)

> Explain that the purpose of Active Listening is to slow down the conversation, so that the listener(s) take time to really hear what the other person is saying, rather than thinking about what they are going to say. This is important because a) everyone likes to be heard (and careful listening is a sign of respect and caring) and b) sometimes there are misunderstandings, so repeating back what the speaker has said helps to eliminate misunderstandings.

B. Feelings Assessment

In addition to its use in ongoing therapy, the *Feelings Check-Up* can be used during the first therapy session with a child as part of an overall assessment and as an introduction to therapy.

1. Assessment

For example, toward the end of the session, in talking about what to expect from therapy, the therapist can say something like:

> *I want you to think of three emotions you would like to have more of in your life, and three emotions you would like to have less of. Draw a star next to the three emotions that you would like to have more of and put a X next to the three that you would like to have less of.*

Once the client has identified the emotions, the therapist can gather information about the circumstances where those emotions are typically experienced. This information can then be used to set some tentative goals for therapy and to ask for the child's agreement to work on those goals.

> *So, you would like to feel more* **proud,** *like when you make a good grade on a test, and more* **happy**, *like when your family plays games together, and more* **relaxed** *like you feel when you do on the weekend when you don't have to go to school. And you'd like to feel less* **annoyed**, *like when your brother comes in your room, and less* **anxious** *and* **stressed,** *like when you have too much homework or when you have a test. Is that right?*

2. Introduction to therapy

> *One of the things that I do with kids is help them figure out ways to feel more relaxed, and less anxious and stressed.*

The therapist can then give some examples of the types of interventions to expect in the therapy. The page can be kept and referred to at future sessions as a method of occasionally assessing progress towards those goals and/or setting new goals.

Speak from the Heart *Word* Finder
Put your Feelings into *Words*

Be a feelings detective: Find the words that best express your emotions.

Happy
pleased
proud
confident
calm
sympathetic
friendly
loved
understood
fortunate
excited

hopeful
content
optimistic
appreciated

Sad
left out
unhappy
sorrowful
discouraged

blue
lonely
guilty
ashamed
embarrassed
remorseful
disappointed
hopeless
depressed
miserable

Unsure
nervous
worried
scared
shy
insecure
suspicious
surprised
shocked
mixed-up
confused

anxious
stressed
afraid
uneasy

Mad
annoyed
disapproving
fed-up
jealous
determined
defiant
disgusted
frustrated
angry
furious

impatient
outraged
offended
aggravated

SHOW ME HOW YOU FEEL

Rationale:
When young children act out in response to upsetting events, they are often directed to "use their words" to express their emotions. To follow this directive, the child needs to be able to internally process their emotional reactions and then translate that understanding into words. This is beyond the ability of many young children. In this activity, a chart is used to help the young child better identify emotions and then convey that information to others.

Application/Treatment Modality: Individual or family therapy with young children (pre-K through early elementary school). This activity can also be used with groups.

Goals:
With this activity, young children:
- learn to use the *Feelings Word Finder* as a tool to identify their emotions, using both pictures and words
- recognize the connection between situations and consequent emotions.
- recognize that feelings can change as the situation changes.

Materials Needed:
1. *Feelings Word Finder* (Junior version) (page 18)
2. *Here's What Happened* cards (Junior version) (page 19)
3. Puppets and/or stuffed animals

A. Introduce the *Feelings Word Finder*.

1. Show the child the *Word Finder* and ask the child to look at the faces. Tell the child:
   We have lots of different kinds of feelings. Sometimes we have happy feelings.

2. Ask the child to point to the *section* that has happy feelings. Do the same with Sad, Worried, and Mad, having the child point to the **sections** on the chart.
   Our feelings can be big feelings or they might be small feelings. One day I might feel a little bit happy and the next day my happy feeling might be really big. There are different names for happy feelings, too.

3. Then go over each section. For example:
   This word says HAPPY. When did you feel happy?

4. As you go through each section, also ask if the child knows any other words for happy (or sad, etc.) If the child offers other words, write them in that section. Move at the child's pace. With some children, identifying just one word for each section may be enough.

B. Practice using the *Feelings Word Finder* with the *Here's What Happened* cards (Junior Version)

1. Read the cards in order (A1, A2, A3, A4). See example at right.

2. As you read each card, have the child use the chart to "show" what emotions the person* (see note below) described on the card might be feeling.

   The child may answer in words only (happy, excited, or scared). If so, ask the child to indicate the intensity ("show how big that feeling is") by pointing to one of the faces.

A boy named Bo goes to school. It is his first day. He already met his teacher and she is nice. But he doesn't know any of the other children.

3. Before moving on to the next card, ask:
   Do you think Bo might have any other feelings on his first day of school?

   If the child replies, go through the same process as above. Asking for other feelings helps the child to understand that we may experience "mixed" emotions.

4. Repeat this process with the other cards as appropriate for the child's maturity and interest level.

At circle time, the Teacher asks Bo to come and sit right next to her.

*Note: there are three sets of cards. The first is about Bo; the second is about Allie. In the 3rd set of cards, the person highlighted shifts among the two children (Max and Sara), and also their sitter and their father. This allows the child to view one situation from multiple perspectives.

After introducing the *Feelings Word Finder* through the preceding activities, the chart can then be used to help children identify, and better understand, their own emotional reactions to events in their lives.

C. Use the *Word Finder* to help children identify their own emotions

1. Talk about the event and have the child identify the primary emotion and its intensity. For example, the therapist might say:

   Show me how you felt when your friend took away your toy.

   If the child points to one of the faces in the "mad" section, the therapist can ask the child to name the feeling. If the child does not name the feeling, that is OK; the therapist can just identify the feeling by labeling the size of the feeling:

   You are pointing to this mad face; it sounds like you had a big mad feeling when your friend took your toy.

2. The therapist might also ask if the child was feeling any of the other emotions at the time, thus helping the child recognize that people can have "mixed emotions."

   Sometimes people feel more than one feeling at the same time. Did you have any of other feelings when your friend took your toy?

   The child may also have experienced feelings of sadness and/or worry in response to his friend's behavior.

   So, you felt a big mad feeling and also a small sad feeling.

D. Help the child to "think" about their feelings

Once the child is able to accurately identify his or her own emotional reactions to events, the therapist can help the child express some of the beliefs/thoughts associated with those emotions.

1. One way to help the child express these thoughts is to ask questions such as:

   What were you thinking when you were feeling that big mad feeling?"
   What were you saying to yourself in your head when you were feeling that little sad feeling?

   For example, the therapist might help the child explain that he was feeling "big" anger because he wanted to play with the toy himself, and also a "little" sad because he thought his friend was being mean to him and/or did not like him.

2. Another way to help children identify thoughts that underlie their emotions is to use puppets. For example, the therapist might choose a puppet to represent a child who has had something taken away by a friend.

   This puppy had the same thing happen to him. Another puppy took his bone away."

   • The therapist then asks the child to pick some other puppets "who saw what happened." (Encourage the child to pick a variety of puppets–a kitten, a turtle, and a wolf, for example).

   • The therapist then uses the "puppy" to talk with each of the observers. Have the child use the other puppets to explain what happened, why it happened, and what each one thinks the puppy should do.

   > Note: This process provides a way for the child to examine the event from more than one perspective. It may also reveal "hidden" thoughts that the child might not reveal in a normal conversation.

   • The therapist can also switch puppets with the child, giving the puppy to the child. The therapist can then take on the role of observer and reflecting on the situation from different perspectives. The therapist can thus model cognitive flexibility. The ability to be flexible in thinking about emotionally charged events paves the way for developing strategies for coping with challenging emotions; this will be expanded on in the upcoming section: *Are You a Careful Thinker?*

Speak from the Heart

Word **Finder**  STOP

..and tell me how you feel.

HAPPY

loving

excited

calm

SAD

disappointed

sorry

lonely

surprised

shy

worried

SCARED

frustrated

annoyed

jealous

MAD

How to make the HERE'S WHAT HAPPENED cards:
1. Print this page (card fronts).
2. If desired, on the reverse side of these cards, you can print the "Here's What Happened" card backs (Page 12)
3. Cut along the dotted lines to make cards.

A boy named **Bo** goes to school. It is his first day. He already met his teacher and she is nice. But he doesn't know any of the other children.

A1

At circle time, the teacher asks **Bo** to come and sit right next to her.

A2

It's lunch time and they are having spaghetti. At home, **Bo**'s mom fixes his spaghetti plain, with just butter and cheese. But this spaghetti has tomato sauce on it.

A3

On the playground, **Bo** was playing with the ball. A girl came up to him and asked, "Can I play with you?"

A4

Allie likes to sleep with her mother. Her mother says that she is too big now and that she has to sleep in her own room.

B1

Allie is sleeping by herself in her room and she hears a noise. She calls her mom and her mom says the noise is just a branch scraping on the window.

B2

Allie's mom says she has a good idea. She puts on some soft music for Allie to listen to while she is falling asleep. Allie can still hear the branch, though.

B3

The next day, Allie's mom cuts off the branch that is scraping on the window. **Allie** puts the branch in her sand-box and pretends it's a tree for her doll.

B4

Sara's dad says that she can watch her favorite show after school. Her brother Max says that it's a baby show.

C1

Sara's babysitter says that she likes the show that Sara wants to watch. She says that she'll watch it with Sara.

C2

Max reminds the sitter that she said she'd play soccer. She tells him to look outside-- it's raining.

C3

Max can't play outside be-cause it's raining. Sara and the babysitter are watching a show. When he looks at his sister, she makes a face at him.

C4

The **sitter** says she will play a board game. When Max starts to lose, he throws all the game pieces on the floor. Sara hits him. The sitter sends them to their rooms.

C5

When their **dad** comes home, he asks why Sara and Max are in their rooms. The sitter says that they have been mean to one another.

C6

Max tells **Sara** that they should apologize to the sitter. They do. They pick up the game. Their dad smiles and the sitter says they can try again tomorrow.

C7

BE A FEELINGS DETECTIVE

Rationale:
An important component of CBT is learning 1) to distinguish between **facts** and **beliefs** and 2) to challenge and re-frame beliefs that are irrational and/or unhelpful. This assignment gives the child practice in making that distinction.

Application/Treatment modality: Home assignment
Note: Home assignments are often part of CBT and help clients to take the information learned in the therapy session and apply it to real-life situations. Clients are more likely to follow through on an assignment if the therapist puts it in writing and gives "hands-on" materials to be brought back to the next therapy session.

Goals:
With this activity, children:

- recognize the connection between situations and consequent emotions.
- practice identifying only the "facts" of situations, without including thoughts or beliefs about the situation.

Materials Needed:
1. **Be a Feelings Detective** (page 22, a variation of Feelings Word Finder)
2. Sample **Here's What Happened** cards (pages 7-10)
3. Make-your-own **Here's What Happened** cards (page 23)

Review some of the sample *Here's What Happened* cards.

2. Point out that the card tell about things that happen to people and that they describe only the "facts" about what happened. Explain:
> **Facts** are things that a detective could observe if he or she were standing right there when it happened.

For example, one card reads:
> *At recess, Julie's friend tells her that she doesn't want to play with her.*

Explain to the child:
> *We don't know why the friend said she wouldn't play with Julie. Julie might **think** that her friend is mad at her; but there could another reason. Maybe her friend is not feeling well and wants to sit and rest. The detective can't see inside of the friend's mind and know **why** she doesn't want to play. The detective can only report the **facts**: At recess, Julie's friend tells her that she doesn't want to play with her.*

3. Give the child a copy of *Be a Feelings Detective* to take home. Ask the child to circle feelings that they observe in themselves and others and, on the back of the page, to write down the situation that gave rise to each feeling.

In writing "what happened" the child should think like a detective, and only write down the "facts" –things that can be seen and/or heard. Tell the child that at the next session, they will use those facts to make some new *Here's What Happened* cards.

Follow-up

1. When the *Word Finder* is returned, have the child review the emotions and the situations that gave rise to them.

2. Invite the child to make new *Here's What Happened* cards, based on the events they recorded. Before writing, children may first need help sorting out the events that led to the emotions.

Your father yells at you and makes you go to your room when you don't turn off the TV.

> For example, Evan's chart indicated that he felt **mad**, **angry**, **sad** and **left out**. On the back of the chart Evan had written: *My dad was mean to me.*

> The therapist questioned Evan and learned that "being mean" meant that his father yelled at him and sent him to his room and that this happened when Evan did not turn off the TV as instructed.

> This more detailed and factual explanation of the situation can be used to create a card (see sample at right)

3. To further expand on this activity, the therapist might also encourage Evan to make another card, this one from his father's (or another family member's) point of view:

> *You tell your son to turn off the TV and come and sit down for dinner. He doesn't do it.*

You tell your son to turn off the TV and come and sit down for dinner. He doesn't do it.

4. Evan could then use this card and the *Feelings Word Finder* to show how a father in this situation might feel. (See card at right.) This can help the child to be more flexible in the way he thinks about the situation. (Cognitive flexibility is one of the primary goals of CBT.)

NOTE: Cards that the child makes in this assignment can:
- be incorporated into clinical interventions planned for that day's session
- be saved to assess progress.
- be used with other tools in this manual, such as *The Stressometer* and *Be a Careful Thinker*.

Speak from the Heart *Word* **Finder**

Put your **Feelings** into *Words*

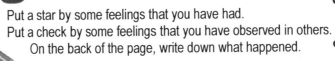

Be a feelings detective:

Put a star by some feelings that you have had.
Put a check by some feelings that you have observed in others.
On the back of the page, write down what happened.

Happy

pleased
proud
confident
calm
sympathetic
friendly
loved
understood
fortunate
excited

hopeful
content
optimistic
appreciated

Sad

left out
unhappy
sorrowful
discouraged

blue
lonely
guilty
ashamed
embarrassed
remorseful
disappointed
hopeless
depressed
miserable

Unsure

nervous
worried
scared
shy
insecure
suspicious
surprised
shocked
mixed-up
confused

anxious
stressed
afraid
uneasy

Mad

annoyed
disapproving
fed-up
jealous
determined
defiant
disgusted
frustrated
angry
furious

impatient
outraged
offended
aggravated

HERE'S WHAT HAPPENED cards (Make Your Own)

How to make your own HERE'S WHAT HAPPENED cards:
1. Copy this page (card backs).
2. Cut along the dotted lines to make cards.
3. Write a situation on the other side of each card.

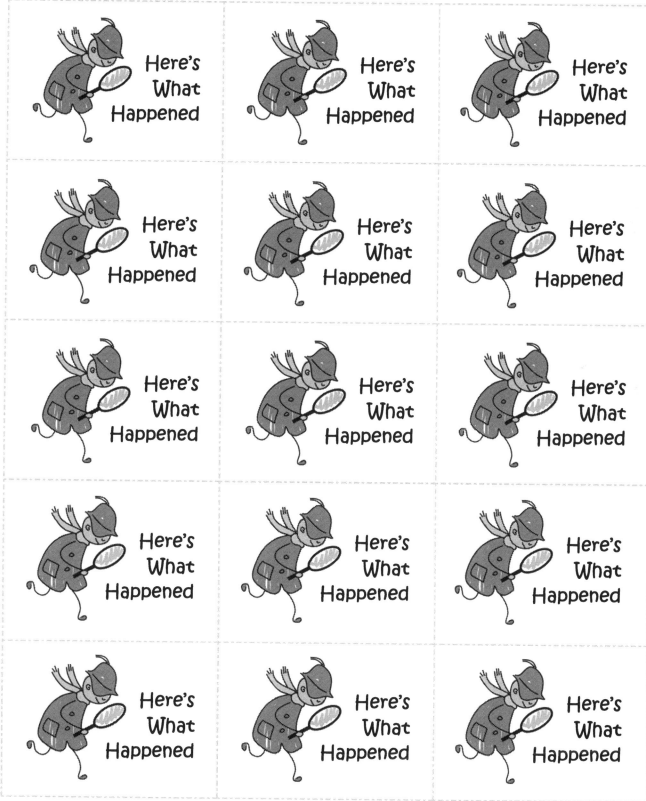

THE STRESSOMETER

Rationale:

Stress is a natural part of life and some stress can actually be good for us--it's called **healthy stress.** However, too many stressors and/or too few effective strategies for coping with stress results in **unhealthy stress.** It is helpful for children to be able to accurately identify not only the sources of stress (the stressors) in their lives but also to be able to measure their personal stress level, assessing where they fall on the healthy-unhealthy stress continuum.

Application/Treatment modality: This activity is intended to be an assessment tool for individual therapy.

Goals:

With this activity children:
• learn the difference between healthy and unhealthy stress.
• use the *Stressometer* as a tool to assess the impact of stress on their lives.
• learn about the role of therapy in helping them deal with stress.

Materials Needed:

1. *Stress Can Be Good - Sometimes!* (Page 26)
2. *The Stressometer* (Page 27)
3. Blank *Here's What Happened* cards (Page 23)

1. Begin with a discussion of **healthy** and **unhealthy** stress. (See *Stress Can Be Good - Sometimes!*)

2. Help the child to identify a number of stressors in his or her life. Try to include examples of both healthy and unhealthy stress. (Optional: write them on blank *Here's What Happened* cards.)

3. Introduce *The Stressometer* and ask the child to choose *one* of the stressors to talk about. (It might be a good idea to begin with healthy stress before tackling the more challenging situations.) The Stressometer has two parts:

Part 1: the feelings chart, used to explore the child's emotional response to a specific stressor.

Part 2: the stress thermometer, used to assess how well the child is coping with that stressor, and whether they are experiencing **healthy** or **unhealthy** stress (or somewhere in between).

Part 1: Using the feelings chart, have the child identify the emotions associated with the selected stressor. Take time with this (especially as you move on to the more challenging situations), allowing the child to fully explore their emotions, which are likely to be mixed.

The same stressor may cause varying types and levels of emotions at different times, depending on a variety of factors, including the support and coping strategies that are available. For example, if a child selects the situation "My parents fight and yell at one another," the child may feel *worried* on some occasions, but *angry* on others. The child may feel *sad* every time their parents fight, but also feel *relieved* and *loved* when a older sibling is there to provide comfort.

Analyzing the emotions with this level of detail, and including information about healthy coping strategies and support, will provide valuable information needed for the next step.

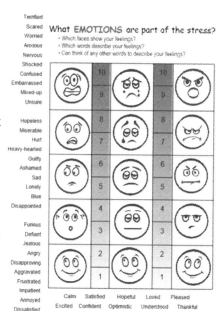

How BIG is the stress?
• Use the thermometer to show how intense the emotions are.

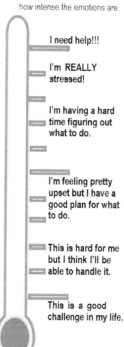

I need help!!!

I'm REALLY stressed!

I'm having a hard time figuring out what to do.

I'm feeling pretty upset but I have a good plan for what to do.

This is hard for me but I think I'll be able to handle it.

This is a good challenge in my life.

Part 2: Using the stress thermometer, help the child assess his or her stress level (with regard to that particular stressor) and determine whether the stress that they are experiencing is healthy stress, unhealthy stress, or somewhere in between.

As you discuss the various levels of stress with the child, you can gather additional information about the coping strategies (including accessing support) that they have been using.

Thank the child for their hard work. If they have revealed significant stress, remind them that your role is to help them find a plan to keep their stress at a healthy level.

Follow up: Let the child know that the purpose of this assessment process is to lay a foundation for therapeutic interventions designed to:
• eliminate or transform some of the stressors in the child's life;
• support the development of healthy methods of coping with stress.

The next tool, *Top 4 Stress Busters* can be used to explain to children what to expect in therapy.

Stress can be good - sometimes

Did you know that not all stress is bad? Although too much stress is unhealthy, some stress is actually healthy and good for us.

• For example, it is natural to feel excitement along with a bit of uncertainty or anxiety in a new situation or before a taking a test, participating in a competition, or performing in public. While we might wish we could get rid of the butterflies in our stomach, those butterflies are a sign of healthy stress. They mean that our bodies are preparing us to be on alert so that we can do our best in the upcoming situation.

• Similarly, when we learn a new skill we may feel some annoyance or frustration as we struggle to get it right. But in small doses, those feelings can give us the determination and focus to continue trying until we experience success.

• Even the stress that we experience when decidedly unpleasant things happen to us serves a healthy function: it is a sign that our bodies and minds are preparing us to take some sort of action in response to the unpleasant event. Without it, we would not have the motivation to do something to protect ourselves or others from harm.

In summary, **healthy stress** helps us be ready to do what we need to do in challenging situations and--when we succeed--leaves us feeling confident in ourselves and our abilities.

Unhealthy stress has the opposite effect: instead of helping us to do the things we need to do, unhealthy stress makes it harder. Unhealthy stress occurs when the stressful situations overwhelm our confidence.

Rather than feeling prepared to meet the challenge, we have strong feelings of anxiety, grief, and/or anger along with physical symptoms such as rapid heart beat, sweaty palms, headaches, stomachaches, listlessness, agitation and more.

We have a hard time knowing what to do and, in our confusion, we may choose to do things that make the stress worse.

The thermometer at the right shows different levels of stress, from healthy to unhealthy.

• At the bottom of the thermometer, it says *This (stressor) is a good challenge in my life. I feel confident!* This is a **healthy** level of stress.

• Moving up the thermometer it says -- *This is hard for me but I think I'll be able to handle it.* This is still a fairly healthy level of stress, because even though it's hard, I think I'll probably be able to meet the challenge.

• Moving further up it says-- *I'm feeling pretty upset but I have a good plan for what to do.* At this level, I'm upset: I have strong feelings and maybe I have some physical symptoms. But I have a plan for what to do to make things better, so that helps me feel less stressed.

• As we move further up it says -- *I'm having a hard time figuring out what to do.* This is moving into unhealthy levels of stress and I may even do things that make the stress worse.* Maybe talking with someone else will help me think about things differently and come up with a plan.

• Moving toward the top of the thermometer, the upset feelings are really strong. This is **unhealthy stress** because I just can't figure out a way to make things better. It's definitely time to tell myself *I'm really stressed and I need some help!*

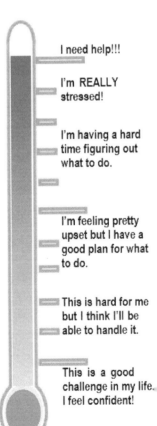

I need help!!!

I'm REALLY stressed!

I'm having a hard time figuring out what to do.

I'm feeling pretty upset but I have a good plan for what to do.

This is hard for me but I think I'll be able to handle it.

This is a good challenge in my life. I feel confident!

*When people reach high levels of stress, they may do things that make them feel better for a while but that really just cause more stress (like eating too much or not enough, sleeping too much or not enough, staying in their room, avoiding people, or taking their frustration out on other people.) When someone gets to this level of stress, it's **very important** to figure out how to get back to a healthy level.

The STRESSOMETER

What is a situation that causes stress in your life?

What EMOTIONS are part of the stress?
- Which faces show your feelings?
- Which words describe your feelings?
- Can think of any other words to describe your feelings?

Terrified
Scared
Worried
Anxious
Nervous
Shocked
Confused
Embarrassed
Mixed-up
Unsure

Hopeless
Miserable
Hurt
Heavy-hearted
Guilty
Ashamed
Sad
Lonely
Blue
Disappointed

Furious
Defiant
Jealous
Angry
Disapproving
Aggravated
Frustrated
Impatient
Annoyed
Dissatisfied

	10 9		10 9	
	8 7		8 7	
	6 5		6 5	
	4 3		4 3	
	2 1		2 1	

Calm   Satisfied   Hopeful   Loved   Pleased

Excited   Confident   Optimistic   Understood   Thankful

How BIG is the stress?
- Use the thermometer to show how intense the emotions are.

I need help!!!

I'm REALLY stressed!

I'm having a hard time figuring out what to do.

I'm feeling pretty upset but I have a good plan for what to do.

This is hard for me but I think I'll be able to handle it.

This is a good challenge in my life.

TOP 4 STRESS-BUSTERS

Rationale:
It is important for children who are in therapy to understand what therapy is all about, what the therapist will do, what the child is expected to do, and what the parents will do.

Application/Treatment modality: Individual and family therapy.

Goals:
With this activity, children:
- learn that they can cope with stressful situations and difficult emotions by learning strategies and skills.
- are introduced to four categories of CBT skills (*Stress Busters*) that will be learned in therapy.
- make a commitment to being an active participant in the treatment plan.

Materials Needed:
1. *Top 4 Stress-Busters* handout (Page 29)
2. Optional: The Stressometer and/or personal *Here's What Happened* cards (created by the child in previous activities).

Each of the four *Stress Busters* corresponds with a CBT concept and with one of the activities in Section II		
Stress Buster	**CBT concept**	**Section II Activity**
1. STOP doing things that aren't helpful	Response inhibition	*Don't Do It!* activities Pages 31-36
2. CHOOSE the best way of thinking	Cognitive flexibility	*Are You a Careful Thinker?* activities Pages 37-53
3. CALM your body	Physiological arousal, monitoring, self-calming	*Slow Down and Get Calm* Pages 53-56
4. Make a PLAN	Cognitive flexibility, problem solving	*What's the Problem, What's the Plan?* Pages 57-63

Instructions

1. Summarize some of the stressors that the child has identified in previous activities (such as *The Stressometer* or *Be A Feelings Detective*). If desired, you can refer to the *Here's What Happened* cards that the child has made.

2. Tell the child that in future therapy sessions, you will help the child learn some strategies to keep their stress at a healthy level. Using the *Top 4 Stress-Busters* handout, explain that there are four main strategies to be learned. Acknowledge that learning to use the strategies may be hard at times; doing things in a new way can be a big challenge.

3. In CBT, the child is expected to be an active partner in the treatment plan. It may be helpful to explain the roles of the people involved in the child's therapy. For example:
- The therapist teaches the four strategies in therapy sessions: that part will be fun!
- Then the child is expected to use the four strategies in their day-to-day life.
- If the child has difficulty the therapist will help them think of ways make it easier. For example, the therapist can give them something to take home as a reminder of what to do. The child can also ask the parents to give them a cue that will help them remember what to do.
- Everyone wants the child to succeed in using the stress-busters. They will be a team: therapist, child and parents.

Top 4
Stress-Busters

 **1. STOP** doing things that aren't helpful.

2. CHOOSE the best way of thinking.

 **3. CALM** your body.

4. Make a good **PLAN.**

Part II:

Tools to help children understand and regulate emotions and behavior

DON'T DO IT!

Rationale:

It can be difficult to apply the principles of CBT in everyday life because we may habitually respond to a given situation with an automatic response that is not helpful. In order to try out new responses, we have to first be aware of, and then inhibit, this automatic response. This activity uses two traditional childhood games: Simon Says and Red-Light, Green-Light. Although these games are simple and fun, what is being practiced--***response inhibition***--is an ability that is essential for emotional and behavioral regulation. As children demonstrate this ability within the structure of a game, they become aware that they can make a conscious choice to control their self-talk and their actions.

Application/Treatment modality: Individual, family, group

Goals:

With this activity, children:
- demonstrate their ability to ***inhibit actions*** that are not appropriate or helpful to a given situation.
- practice using self-talk (the words *Don't Do It*) to support their intentions and guide their behavior.
- reflect on the importance of this ability in their everyday lives and identify situations in which they might benefit from response inhibition.

Materials Needed:
1. ***Don't Do It!*** poster (Page 35)
2. ***Don't Do It!*** cards (Page 36)

Introduce the activities by explaining response inhibition:
*Sometimes what we don't do is just as important as what we do. That's because we have to stop ourselves from doing things that aren't right or aren't helpful. Sometimes it's really hard to stop ourselves, and we have to tell ourselves **Don't Do It!***

Place the ***Don't Do It*** poster in a spot where the child can look at it during the activity.
*Can you think of times that it's important to tell yourself **Don't Do It** and stop yourself from doing something?*

If the child doesn't offer any examples, that's OK; just continue with the activity and get back to the question later. Tell the child:
We are going to play some games so you can show me how good you are at stopping yourself.

GAME #1: Red Light, Green Light (interrupting an ongoing response)

1. In this game, the therapist is the Stop Light and stands at one end of the room. The child stands at the opposite end.

2. When the Stop Light says "**Green Light**," the child can walk, hop on one foot, jump, skip, or crawl (no running unless played outdoors) toward the Stop Light.

3. At any time, the Stop Light can say "**Red Light**." Then the child has to STOP completely and immediately, even if in mid-movement. If the child moves at all after **Red Light** is called, they have to go back to the beginning.

4. Then the Stop Light says **Green Light** and the child can move again until the next time **Red Light** is called.
    Suggestion: To make this game more challenging (and silly), sometimes use similar sounding words for Green Light and Red Light. (Green Grass, Green Tight, Red Bed, Red Fight.)

5. The game is complete when the child reaches the Stop Light. Then the child has a turn to be the Stop Light.

    VARIATION: If there is not enough space to move across the room, the child can engage in some sort of activity, for example building with blocks, or putting together a puzzle or doing a dance. They begin when the Stop Light says ***Green Light*** and must stop in mid-movement when they hear the cue ***Red Light***. Since there is no clear end point in this game, just play for a while and when the child shows mastery, and then switch roles.

(Continued on next page)

Don't Do It! Instructions - Continued

GAME #2: Simon Says Don't Do It (preemptively stopping an automatic response)

Set-up for the game:
"Simon" (the therapist) stands on one side of the room (Finish Line) and the child stands on the other end (Start Line.)

Tell the child:
> *When we played Red Light, Green Light, stopped yourself in the middle of doing something, Now we are going to play Simon Says. With this game, you have to stop yourself before you even start to do something.*

> *The name of this activity is **Simon Says Don't Do It!** In this game, what you **Don't Do** is very, very important.*

Simon Says Don't Do It, Part 1
1. The rules of the game are:
   - Simon gives commands such as *Take a baby step, Take a giant step, Take a medium step, Take a bunny hop*
   - Sometimes Simon begins the command with the magic words, **Simon Says.**
   - Sometimes Simon gives the command without saying the magic words.
   - The child is to follow the command *only* when it is preceded by the magic words, **Simons Says**.
   - If the child follows the command without the magic words, they have to go back to Start and begin again.

   > **Note:** Go slowly and give the child a chance to succeed. However, try to "trick" the child into taking at least one wrong move, so that he has the experience of going back to the Start Line. Try to do this early on and then follow up more slowly, giving the child a chance to succeed. If the child starts to do the "wrong thing" and then stops himself, comment on this: *Good job! You remembered and you stopped yourself.*

2. If time allows, give the child a chance to be Simon before moving on to the next part of the game.

Simon Says Don't Do It, Part 2
1. Begin by giving the child a *Don't Do It!* Card
   > *We are going to play **Simon Says** again and we are going to do a few things differently. It's going to be a little harder to win because I am going to try really, really hard to trick you. Also, whenever I tell you to do something without saying the magic words **Simon Says**, I want you to look at your Don't Do It! card and whisper to yourself, "**Don't do it!**"*

2. Have the child practice doing this. The whisper needs to be loud enough for you to hear. Tell the child:
   > *If you move at the wrong time **OR** if you forget to look at the card and whisper "Don't Do It!" you will have to go back to the start line.*

3. In this version, Simon tries harder to trick the child. Some ways to do this are:
   - Sometimes begin the command with similar but different words
     (*Slimon Says, Pimon Says, Simon Suggests, Simon wants you to......*)
   - Sometimes begin with the child's name (*Marie, take one giant step forward.*)
   - Say, *Let's do this,* and demonstrate a funny or silly move.

4. Practice together. Feel free to ham it up and be silly; make it fun, even if the child has to start over again. For example, the two of you might practice saying **Don't Do It** in three different kinds of voices.

   > Note: The purpose of this game is to have the child use "self-talk" as an aid to inhibiting behavior.
   > Respond to their actions in ways that raise their awareness of their ability to do this.
   > - If the child remembers to whisper **Don't Do It**, be sure to acknowledge this:
   >   *Good job, you told yourself just what to do...*
   > - If the child starts to do the "wrong thing" and then stops and whispers **Don't Do It**, comment on this:
   >   *Good job! You told yourself to **stop** just in time.*
   > - If the child fails to inhibit his behavior, or fails to whisper **Don't Do It**, comment on this:
   >   *Uh-oh, what did you forget to do? It's back to the starting line!*
   >   *Let's practice. What do we need to tell ourselves when there is something we are not supposed to do?*

5. If time allows, the child may enjoy a turn to be Simon. Also, it can be helpful and a lot of fun, to have the parent join the child and therapist in playing the games.

DON'T DO IT! - Home Assignment

Rationale:
It can be difficult to apply the principles of CBT in everyday life because we may habitually respond to a given situation with an automatic response that is not helpful. Most children can readily understand the *need* to inhibit certain behaviors in everyday life. However, being able to actually inhibit those habitual responses can be very difficult (even for adults). Everyone can benefit from interventions designed to foster motivation and bolster good intentions.

Application/Treatment modality: Family therapy session (Can be adapted for individual session)

Goals:
With this activity, children:
- discuss the importance of **inhibiting actions** that are not appropriate or helpful to a given situation.
- receive encouragement and support from therapist and parent(s)
- reflect on the importance of this ability in their everyday lives and identify situations in which they might benefit from response inhibition
- make a commitment to trying to eliminate at least one unwanted behavior.

Materials Needed:
Don't Do It! Cards (Page 36)

Instructions

After playing the *Don't Do It!* Games (pages 29-30) the therapist can help the child recognize the benefits of telling ourselves **"Don't Do It!"** in everyday life.

Note: In this explanation, we will assume that the parents are present for this discussion. However, if that is not possible, the child and therapist can have this discussion and the home assignment can be given to the child to carry out alone.

1. Offer personal examples of the benefits of response inhibitions.
If the child has previously offered an example of when these skills are needed in everyday life, bring that example back into the conversation. For example, if the child has said that they need to refrain from hitting a sibling when the sibling does some annoying thing, discuss the benefits of this response inhibition. Can the child recall a time that they were able to stop? What were the benefits of stopping: for the sibling, for the family, for the child?

The therapist can tell the child that adults as well as children benefit from stopping themselves and offer some examples from his or her everyday life (keeping them simple and generic.) For example:

Yesterday I went to the cabinet and I got out a bag of cookies. I opened the bag up. Then I stopped myself. I remembered that I want to stop eating sweets between meals. Even though I had already opened the bag, I stopped in the middle (just like we did when we played Red-Light, Green Light). Then I closed up the bag and put it back in the cabinet. It was hard, but I felt happy because I know that I will be healthier and feel better if I stop myself form eating sweets between meals.

Note: The preceding example focuses on stopping **one's actions,** as in the games. The next example focuses on stopping **one's thoughts.** Giving the child this type of example will set the stage for the next set of CBT activities: *Are You a Careful Thinker?*

*I was driving and someone pulled right in front of me. I had to slam on my brakes. I started to think what a jerk that person was and that people like that shouldn't be allowed to drive! But then I told myself **Don't Do It!,** just like we did when we played Simon Says. Instead, I thought to myself, "I'm glad I saw him in time to step on the brake." If I had kept thinking about that driver, I would have felt angry and upset. Maybe I would have cursed and pounded on the steering wheel. But I stopped those thoughts and focused on different thoughts. And then I did something that helped me feel much better: I took a deep breath and I turned on some music.*

The child's parents can be asked to offer examples of times in their lives that they need to stop themselves from doing and/or thinking something. Encourage them to also discuss the benefits. Finally, have the child offer some examples of times that he or she could benefit from stopping themselves from doing and/or thinking something. Emphasize the benefits: short and long term, benefits for others as well as for oneself.

(Continued on next page.)

2. Set "Don't Do It" intentions.

An essential step in CBT is planning how to apply the strategies learned in therapy to everyday life. This plan can start with the simple act of having the child make *Don't Do It!* cards to set their intentions. Explain to the family:

It was fun stopping ourselves when we played the games, but in real life it can be hard to stop doing certain things. It's always good to have a reminder, so I want you to think of some things that you want to remember not to do and write them down on these cards.

Provide them with cards and have them each set at least one intention and write it on a card. If they want to do more than one intention, each should be on a separate card.

3. Think of ways to support those intentions.

Children are likely to need a lot of external support to carry out their intentions. Therefore, the child's plan should also include some means of providing that support. One way is to set up "cues" as reminders. Explain to the child what a cue is and say:

The best place to get a cue is at the very moment that we want to stop ourselves from doing something. I made a **Don't Do It!** *card that said "No sweets between meals" and I put it on the cabinet where the cookies are. So when I'm feeling hungry and go to the cabinet to get a cookie, the cue is right there to remind me to stop. What about you; can you think of a good place to put your card so that it can be a reminder?*

Help the family to brainstorm for ideas of where to place the card so it can be a cue. If the situation doesn't lend itself having a visual reminder, suggest that the card be put somewhere where the child will see it in the morning. Then talk about other types of "cues" that family members can give to one another.

The cards are one type of cue to help us remember our intentions. One nice thing about being part of a family is that we can help one another remember what it is we are trying to do. Is there is a way that someone in your family can give you a signal that can be a cue for you stop yourself?

Have the family brainstorm for ideas. For example, perhaps the words *Red Light* could be a verbal cue. Or, they may prefer some other sort of "secret signal." Whatever the plan, emphasize that this is the child's plan: 1) the child has set an intention to refrain from some habitual response; 2) the child has outlined the benefits to come from following through on this intention; and 3) the child has planned for (and perhaps asked for) support in carrying out this plan.

As with any home assignment, it is important that the therapist follow up at the next session, celebrate if the child has been successful, and provide trouble-shooting and encouragement if the child had difficulty following through.

ARE YOU A CAREFUL THINKER?

Rationale:
Cognitive restructuring is a core component of CBT in which the client
1) identifies the unhelpful thoughts, faulty assumptions, and irrational beliefs that accompany unhealthy stress and
2) formulates alternative ways of thinking that are more accurate and helpful. This promotes cognitive flexibility.

Typically, this restructuring begins during therapy sessions, in the context of a dialog between the therapist and client. In working with child clients, it can be difficult to hold a child's attention for conversations of this sort, so strategies to make the process more concrete and hands-on are helpful.

Application/Treatment modality: Individual, family, group

Goals:
With this activity, children:
- learn that by changing the way they think about a stressful situation, they can change the outcome.
- develop cognitive flexibility by brainstorming for "helpful thoughts."

Materials Needed:
1. *Top 4 Stress-Busters* (Page 29)
2. *I Can Choose!* diagram (Page 40)
3. *Be a Careful Thinker* (Page 41)
4. *Here's What Happened* cards (When demonstrating the *I Can Choose* diagram with a child the first time, you will need both one sample card from page 42 and also one card that the child created for the **The Stressometer** activity. For the child's card, choose one that involved a moderate amount of distress.)

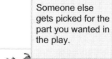

Step 1: BRIEF INTRODUCTION TO THE *I Can Choose* DIAGRAM

1. Review the *Top 4 Stress Busters*. Tell the child:
   This activity is about Stress Buster #2: "Choose the best way of thinking."

2. Remind the child about *Simon Says, Red Light Green Light* and the *Don't Do It!* activities.
   *We talked about stopping yourself from **doing things** that aren't helpful. Sometimes the best way to stop yourself from **doing** unhelpful things is to first stop yourself from **thinking** unhelpful things.*

3. Show the *I Can Choose* diagram.
   This diagram shows a path that splits into two paths. Let's start at the bottom of the path. We are going along in our life, and something happens

4. Place your sample card on the path in the designated spot. (We'll use the card pictured at right as an example, but choose whichever card would be best for your client, or make your own.)
   Let's imagine that I didn't get the part that I wanted in the play, someone else did. And let's also imagine that I got really upset and I said things and I did things that I later regretted.

5. Point to the left arrow and the red stop light there.
   Then I might feel even worse. I may wish I could STOP feeling bad but I just feel stuck where I am.

6. Go back to the start of the diagram.
   A lot of people don't know that just by finding a different way to think about what happened, we can avoid feeling stuck in upsetting feelings.

7. Point to the arrow on the right side of the diagram.
   By thinking about the situation in the right way, we can feel more calm and ready to deal with what is happening. I'm going to show you an example of what I'm talking about.

(Continued on next page.)

Are You a Careful Thinker? Instructions (continued)

Step 2: DEMONSTRATE THE *I Can Choose* DIAGRAM WITH A SAMPLE CARD:

Continuing with the sample card you have chosen, demonstrate the use of the diagram in the following order:

1. Place the card on the path where indicated.

2. Complete the left half of the diagram.
- Give an example of an automatic, unhelpful thought or belief and write it in the thought bubble.
- Ask the child how someone is likely to feel with that thought in their mind. Write the feeling(s) on the path above the bubble.
- Then ask the child how a person might act with those thoughts and feelings. Write the possible actions on the path as as well.

3. Complete the right half of the diagram. Complete in the same order, demonstrating how a more rational and/or helpful perspective can lead to different emotions and actions.

4. Summarize by referring back to the *Top 4 Stress Busters*. Explain to the child that the *I Can Choose* diagram shows a way to use the top two stress busters when you find yourself in a stressful situation:
  1st, stop automatic thoughts that aren't helpful and
  2nd, choosing more helpful thoughts instead. Point out the various parts of the diagram as you explain.

   For example:
   In our example, the stressful situation was that someone else got the part that I really wanted. If my thought or belief about what happened was that it wasn't fair, I would feel angry. I might even quit the theatre group.

   But if I **STOP** *that thought and I look for another way to think about what happened, I find out that there are lots of other ways:*
   - I can think about all the fun I have had meeting new people,
   - I can think about the other things I can do for the play and about the new things I can learn,
   - I can think about what I'll do differently next time there's a try-out for a play.

   If I **CHOOSE** *a more helpful way of thinking, I might still feel disappointed. But I don't feel so angry. And I don't feel so stressed that I want to quit the group.*

Step 3: DEMONSTRATE THE *I Can Choose* DIAGRAM WITH THE CHILD'S SITUATION CARD:

Using a *Here's What Happened* card created by the child, go through the same process with the *I Can Choose* diagram.

1. **Place the card** on the path where indicated.

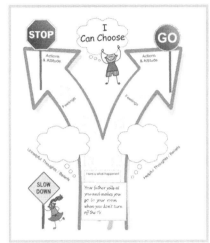

2. **Complete the left half of the diagram.** Begin with the emotions that the child experienced in the stressful situation (write the emotions on the arrow) and then work backward to the thoughts.

> Note: Realize that children may be unaware of some of the automatic thoughts, beliefs and assumptions that underlie their distress. They may need a lot of help in articulating these perceptions. Ask questions: *"I wonder what you were telling yourself when you felt so angry and upset?"* Encourage them to generate several possible thoughts; the more accurately they can identify underlying unhelpful thoughts, the more productive they will be in generating meaningful alternatives. (Older children may benefit from learning about common "thinking traps.")

3. **Complete the right half of the diagram.** After the left side of the diagram has been completed, tell the child:
> *Let's brainstorm for other ways to think about what happened and see if you can find some thoughts that are true and helpful.*

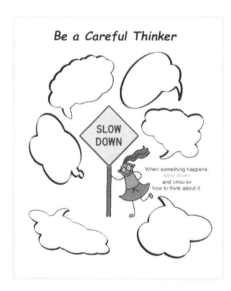

Use the *Be A Careful Thinker* worksheet to brainstorm for alternative perspectives, writing them in the thought bubbles. Encourage the child to fill in *all* of the bubbles: this promotes cognitive flexibility.

After the brainstorming process is complete, have the child select those thoughts that he   or she thinks would be most helpful. Write them on the thought bubble on the right side of diagram. Then complete the rest of the arrow, having the child project how they would feel and act.

4. **Summarize** by referring back to the *Top 4 Stress Busters*. Encourage the child to make a commitment to being a careful thinker and, when stressful things happen, pausing and choosing the best way to think about the situation.

NOTE: Once these materials have been introduced, they can be used in any session to structure CBT discussions.

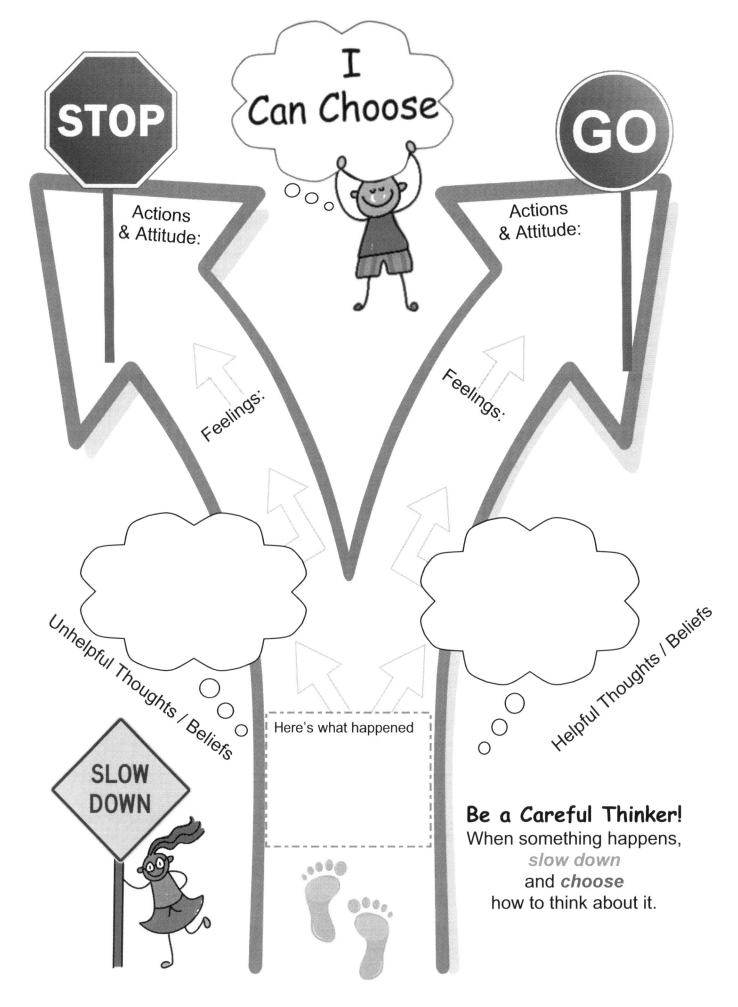

STOP

I Can Choose

GO

Actions & Attitude:

Actions & Attitude:

Feelings:

Feelings:

Unhelpful Thoughts / Beliefs

Helpful Thoughts / Beliefs

Here's what happened

SLOW DOWN

Be a Careful Thinker!
When something happens,
slow down
and *choose*
how to think about it.

Be a Careful Thinker

When something happens, *slow down* and *choose* how to **THINK** about it.

How to make the HERE'S WHAT HAPPENED cards:
1. Copy this page (card fronts).
2. If desired, on the reverse side of these cards, you can copy the "Here's What Happened" card backs (page 12)
3. Cut along the dotted lines to make cards.

You miss the school bus. Your dad yells, *"Not again! I'm not taking you to school this time!"*	You drop a tray of food in the middle of the cafeteria. Everyone laughs.	You were joking around and sort of made fun of your friend. Now your friend won't speak to you.
You tried out for the basketball team. Today is the day that you find out who made the team.	You don't know why the other kids don't want to play with you. Your teacher tells you it is because you always want to be "the boss."	Someone else gets picked for the part you wanted in the play.
You know the answers to all the questions on the test. But you're not finished and the teacher says the time is up.	You aren't paying attention in class. Your teacher calls on you to answer the question.	You got picked for the team. Your best friend didn't and hasn't been talking to you as much.
You are on your way to your band performance. You have to play one part all by yourself.	You forgot to study for the test. You don't know the answers.	You made an A on the test. You tell your dad and your brother says you're always bragging.
Your brother calls you a crybaby.	Your mom says you have to help with chores after school. None of your friends have to do chores after school.	You put your homework on your desk and walk away. When you came back it is gone. You tell the teacher but she says, "No excuses."

Be a MASTERMIND!

Rationale:
An important component of CBT is learning
1) to distinguish between *facts* and **perceptions** (*beliefs, opinions, guesses,* etc.) and
2) to then evaluate those beliefs, opinions and guesses: which are helpful and which are not so helpful?

This activity sets the groundwork for developing *cognitive flexibility*: the ability to "master your mind" and choose the best, most helpful ways of thinking.

Application/Treatment Modality: Home assignment

Goals:
With this activity the child:
- identifies a stressful or challenging situation
- identifies the emotions experienced
- describes the facts of what happened
- identifies subsequent thoughts/perceptions (opinions, beliefs, guesses, etc.)
- evaluates the thoughts: are they helpful or not?

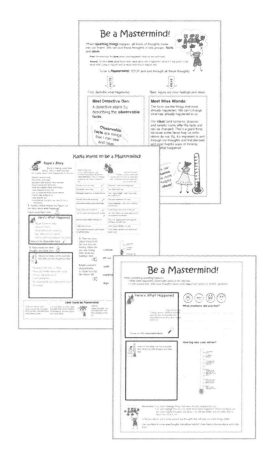

Materials:
Be a Mastermind! (Page 44)
Be a Mastermind example (Kayla Learns to Be a Mastermind) (Page 45)
Be a Mastermind! home assignment form (Page 46)

Instructions

1. Review **Be a Mastermind!**

2. Go over the example (Kayla Learns to Be a Mastermind) on page 45.
   - Begin by reading Kayla's story.
   - Then read the commentary by Detective Dan explaining the difference between the observable facts and Kayla's opinions, beliefs, guesses and feelings.
   - Next, go over the 3-step process that Kayla's mother uses to help her sort through what happened and her subsequent thoughts and feelings.
   - Finally, have the child brainstorm for other, more helpful, ways that Kayla can think about what happened.

3. Give the child a copy of the the Be a Mastermind form (page 46.) Ask that the child take the form home and, when a challenging situation comes along, complete the form. It may be helpful to give the child a copy of Kayla Learns to Be a Mastermind to use as a reference.

Be a Mastermind!

When **upsetting things** happen, all kinds of thoughts come into our minds. We can put these thoughts in two groups: **facts** and **ideas.**

First: We remember the **facts** about what happened: what we saw and heard.

Second: We have **ideas** about those facts: ideas about why it happened, about if it was good or bad, about what's going to happen next or about what *should* happen next.

To be a **Mastermind**, STOP and sort through all those thoughts.

FACTS ⬇

IDEAS ⬇

First, describe what happened:

Next, figure out your ideas and feelings.

Meet Detective Dan:

A detective starts by describing the **observable facts:**

> **Observable facts** are things that I can see and hear.

Facts are different from

ideas · *Opinions*

guesses · BELIEFS · *feelings*

Meet Wise Wanda:

The **facts** are the things that have already happened. We **can't change** what has already happened to us.

Our **ideas** (and opinions, guesses beliefs and feelings) come *after* the facts and **can change.** That's a good thing, because some ideas help us while others do not.

> When we **choose** the most helpful **ideas**, we can stay calm and make wise decisions.

To be a **Mastermind,**

Start by describing the facts.

Then sort through all your other ideas to find the best and most helpful way of thinking about what happened.

Kayla's Story:

Kayla is feeling upset after school. Here is what she told her mother about what happened on the bus:

Ella didn't sit by me today.
Ella sat with Jenna today.
Ella doesn't want to be my friend anymore.
Ella and Jenna were whispering.
Jenna was probably saying mean things.
Casey asked me to sit by her.
I sat by myself and looked out the window.
Everyone was looking at me.
I hate riding the bus!
You should quit your job so you can pick me up from school.

Kayla learns to be a Mastermind!

Detective Dan says:
"I put a magnifying glass 🔍 by all the things Kayla said that are **observable facts**. I drew a line through everything that is **not** an observable fact."

Detective Dan says:
"Feelings, opinions, beliefs and guesses aren't the same as observable facts. Observable facts are things that I can see and/or hear."

Ella didn't sit by me today. 🔍	That's true. I saw Kayla sitting alone.
Ella sat with Jenna today. 🔍	Yep, that's what I saw
~~Ella doesn't want to be my friend anymore.~~	That's Kayla's **belief**. I didn't see or hear any evidence of it.
Ella and Jenna were whispering.. 🔍	They were whispering, it's a fact.
~~Jenna was probably saying mean things.~~	Kayla's **guessing**. I didn't see or hear any evidence of it.
Casey asked me to sit with her. 🔍	I heard Casey invite her to sit with her.
I sat by myself and looked out the window. 🔍	Yes, that's what I saw: Kayla sat by herself and looked out the window.
~~Everyone was probably looking at me.~~	This is her **guess** about what happened. But that is not what I saw.
~~I hate riding the bus!~~	That's Kayla's **feeling**, not a fact.
~~You should quit your job so you can pick me up from school.~~	That's Kayla's **opinion** about what should happen next.

1. Kayla's mother helped her figure out the facts about what happened.

Kayla wrote them here: ⬇1

Here's What Happened

Ella didn't sit by me today.
Ella sat by Jenna.
Ella and Jenna were whispering.
Casey asked me to sit with her.
I sat by myself and looked out the window.

These are the **observable facts**. 🔍

2. Kayla wrote her other thoughts and ideas here: ⬇2

Detective Dan allows only the observable facts! Write your other thoughts and ideas

Ella doesn't want to be my friend.
Jenna was probably saying mean things.
Everyone was looking at me.
I hate riding the bus.
Mom should quit her job so she can pick me up from school!

3. Then her mom asked Kayla to tell her how she was feeling. Kayla wrote her feelings here: ➡3

Kayla colored a stressometer to show how big her stress felt.

➡3

confused

left out

lonely

embarrassed

angry

I need help!!!

I'm REALLY stressed!

I'm having a hard time figuring out what to do.

I'm feeling pretty upset but I have a good plan for what to do.

This is hard for me but I think I'll be able to handle it.

This is a good challenge in my life.

Help Kayla be a Mastermind!

⬆ In the box above, put a circle around any thoughts that you think will help Kayla make things better.

⬆ Can you think of some **new** thoughts that will be helpful? Write them in the box above and circle them.

⬆ With the circled thoughts, how will Kayla feel? Add those feelings to the list.

⬆ With the circled thoughts, how big would Kayla stress feel?

Be a Mastermind!

When something upsetting happens:
- Write what happened (*observable facts*) in the first box.
- In the second box, write your thoughts about what happened (*opinions, beliefs, guesses*).

Here's What Happened

These are the **observable facts**.

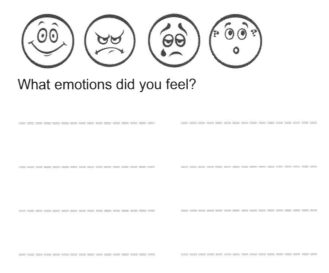

What emotions did you feel?

Detective Dan allows only the observable facts! Write your other thoughts and ideas here:

How big was your stress?

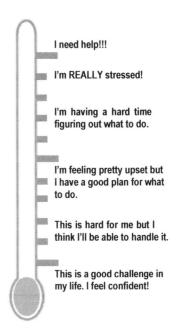

I need help!!!

I'm REALLY stressed!

I'm having a hard time figuring out what to do.

I'm feeling pretty upset but I have a good plan for what to do.

This is hard for me but I think I'll be able to handle it.

This is a good challenge in my life. I feel confident!

In the box above, put a circle around any thoughts that will help you make things better.

Can you think of some **new** thoughts that will be helpful? Write them in the box above and circle them. (You might want to ask someone to help you think of some new thoughts.)

Remember: You **can't change** things that have already happened to you.
You **can change** the way you **think** about what happened. When you use your mind to figure out the most helpful thoughts and ideas, you will feel calmer and be better able to decide what to do.

ARE YOU A CAREFUL THINKER? - Junior Version

Rationale:
Young children often need help in learning to regulate their emotions. The development of **cognitive flexibility**--the ability to think about events from more than one perspective--is essential for emotional regulation. This activity teaches children that they can choose to "think differently" about things that happen and thus bring about a more positive outcome.

Application/Treatment Modality: Ages 4-9, Individual therapy, family therapy.

Goal:
With this activity, young children:
- learn that one's feelings can change if one thinks differently about what has happened.
- are invited to practice being "careful thinkers" in their own lives.

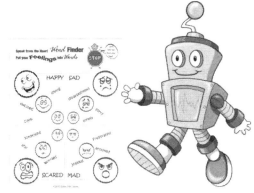

Materials needed:
1) The **Story of Robie-Ro** (Page 48)

2) Feeling Word Finder - Junior Version (Page 18)

3) Something to "mark" the feelings on the chart (such as plastic game markers, poker or bingo chips; even paper clips will work.)

4) *Be a Careful Thinker!* cue card (Page 49)

Instructions

1. Read **The Story of Robie-Ro, Chapter 1** with the child. At the end of the first paragraph, pause after the statement, *That's not fair! They promised I could get a pet.*

2. Using the feeling chart, have the child "show" what kind of emotion(s) Robie might be feeling by placing a marker, chip, etc on top of the corresponding face(s). You can also ask the child to give a name to the feeling. (If the child chooses just one feeling, you might want to ask if Robie could have any other feelings at the same time. This allows the child to represent "mixed" emotions: perhaps he thinks that Robie feels mostly angry, but also sad.)

3. Read the rest of the story, *pausing after each paragraph* so that the child can use the chart and markers (as described above) to show any change in what Robie might be feeling.

4. Read the commentary after Chapter 1, again pausing to help the child reflect on how Robie's feelings might change as his parents talk to him, agree to give him another chance, and come up with a plan.

5. Read Chapter 2. Continue to pause after each paragraph and also at the end of the story, allowing the child to use the chart to mark changes in Robie's emotions as he thinks differently about what has happened.

Follow up:
Even if children are able to easily grasp the concept of "thinking differently" in the therapist's office, that does not mean that they will be able to do so in those real-life situations where they are having difficulty regulating their emotions and behavior. To provide support at home and school:

1) Make a copy of the cue card (page 49) to remind the child of the the skills learned.

2) Arrange for parents and/or teachers to act as coaches to help the child practice the new skills at home and school. As coaches they can:
- provide a "secret signal" that reminds the child to use the skills (as Robie's parents did with the words *Slow Down.*)

- recognize those occasions when the child is successful. (One way to do this is for the coach to make a note on the back of the cue card noting when and where the child was able to use the skills. The child can bring the card back to the therapist.)

- give encouragement to the child on those occasions when they are **not** successful. (*"That's OK. You're still learning. You'll have another chance to be a **Careful Thinker**. I'll give you the secret signal when I see that you are getting upset. Let's practice now."*)

The Story of Robie-Ro

Chapter 1:

On a sunny afternoon, Robie-Ro went out with his parents Mr. and Mrs. Bot. They went to a movie, ate pizza and went shopping. As they were leaving the shopping center, they went by a pet shop. Robie saw the cutest little puppy!. He turned to his father and said "Papa Bot, you told me that some day I could have a pet. That is the one that I want." Mr. Bot said, "Not today, Robie-Ro. We've been out for 3 hours and your mother and I are tired." Well, that wasn't what Robie wanted to hear and the first thought that popped into Robie-Ro's head was: *That's not fair! They promised I could get a pet.*

Robie was so upset that he sat right down in front of the pet shop. His father grabbed his arm and tried to pull him up. Then Robie-Ro thought to himself, *That hurt! They are the meanest parents ever!*

Robie was so upset he started kicking Mr. Bot. Mr Bot looked at Mrs. Bot and said, "The next time we go out, we are leaving him with Sitter Bot." "Good idea," Mrs. Bot said. And that is just what happened. His parents took him home and put him to bed. The next time they went out, they called Sitter Bot to come over to their house and they left Robie-Ro at home.

The End

Did you like the ending of this story? Robie-Ro did not. But after his parents came back home and the sitter left , they talked to Robie and asked him if he would like to learn how to be a *Careful Thinking Robot*. Robie wasn't sure what a Careful Thinking Robot was, but he thought to himself *Sometimes it's fun to learn new things*.

Robie's parents said if he learned about being a careful thinker, they would give him another chance to go out with them. Then they explained what a careful thinker is. They told Robie that when something happens:

1. A careful thinker remembers that the first thought that pops into your head is not always the best one.

2. Then a careful thinker slows down and comes up with some other ways to think about what happened.

3. Then the careful thinker carefully chooses the very best way to think about what happened.

Robie's parents made a plan: They told him: "If we see you start to get upset about something, we will whisper the words, *Slow Down*. Those words will be our secret signal for you to remember to be a *Careful Thinking Robot*."

Chapter 2

Robie-Ro went out with his parents, Mr. and Mrs. Bot. First they went shopping, then they had hamburgers for lunch. Then it was time to go to Grandma-Bot's house. On the way there, they passed by the ice cream shop. Robie-Ro turned to his mother and said "Momma Bot, we didn't have desert after lunch. I want to get an ice cream cone. I'll use my own money!" Mrs. Bot said, "Not today, Robie. Your grandmother is waiting for us." The first though that popped into Robie's head was, *They are so mean, they never get me anything.*

He started to get upset and he made a mean face at Momma-Bot. His mother leaned over and whispered "*Slow Down.*" Then Robie thought *That's our secret signal!*

Robie **remembered** that a Careful Thinker knows that the first thought that pops into your head isn't always the best one. So he took a deep breath and made himself **slow down** to see if he had any other thoughts in his head. Sure enough, there was one. He said to himself, *Well actually, they were very nice to me today. They bought lunch at my favorite restaurant.*

Robie remembered that to be a careful thinker he should choose the best way of thinking about what happened. He didn't want his parents to leave him at home the next time they went out. And his grandma always had cookies at her house. He smiled at his parents and said "Maybe we can get ice cream another day." "Maybe so," said his mom, and smiled back at him. Mr. Bot smiled at both of them.

The End

Be a Careful Thinker!

When something happens:

1. **Remember** that the first thought that pops into your head is not always the best one.

2. **Slow down** and see if there are some other ways to think about what happened.

3. **Carefully choose** the very best way to think about what happened. (You'll be glad you did!)

Be a Careful Thinker!

When something happens:

1. **Remember** that the first thought that pops into your head is not always the best one.

2. **Slow down** and see if there are some other ways to think about what happened.

3. **Carefully choose** the very best way to think about what happened. (You'll be glad you did!)

Be a Careful Thinker!

When something happens:

1. **Remember** that the first thought that pops into your head is not always the best one.

2. **Slow down** and see if there are some other ways to think about what happened.

3. **Carefully choose** the very best way to think about what happened. (You'll be glad you did!)

Be a Careful Thinker!

When something happens:

1. **Remember** that the first thought that pops into your head is not always the best one.

2. **Slow down** and see if there are some other ways to think about what happened.

3. **Carefully choose** the very best way to think about what happened. (You'll be glad you did!)

Be a Careful Thinker!

When something happens:

1. **Remember** that the first thought that pops into your head is not always the best one.

2. **Slow down** and see if there are some other ways to think about what happened.

3. **Carefully choose** the very best way to think about what happened. (You'll be glad you did!)

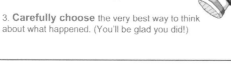

Be a Careful Thinker!

When something happens:

1. **Remember** that the first thought that pops into your head is not always the best one.

2. **Slow down** and see if there are some other ways to think about what happened.

3. **Carefully choose** the very best way to think about what happened. (You'll be glad you did!)

Be a Careful Thinker!

When something happens:

1. **Remember** that the first thought that pops into your head is not always the best one.

2. **Slow down** and see if there are some other ways to think about what happened.

3. **Carefully choose** the very best way to think about what happened. (You'll be glad you did!)

Be a Careful Thinker!

When something happens:

1. **Remember** that the first thought that pops into your head is not always the best one.

2. **Slow down** and see if there are some other ways to think about what happened.

3. **Carefully choose** the very best way to think about what happened. (You'll be glad you did!)

Be a Careful Thinker!

When something happens:

1. **Remember** that the first thought that pops into your head is not always the best one.

2. **Slow down** and see if there are some other ways to think about what happened.

3. **Carefully choose** the very best way to think about what happened. (You'll be glad you did!)

Be a Careful Thinker!

When something happens:

1. **Remember** that the first thought that pops into your head is not always the best one.

2. **Slow down** and see if there are some other ways to think about what happened.

3. **Carefully choose** the very best way to think about what happened. (You'll be glad you did!)

ENCOURAGING WORDS

Rationale:

Cognitive restructuring is a core component of CBT in which the client, with the help of the therapist,

  1) identifies irrational or unhelpful automatic thoughts and

  2) formulates alternative thoughts that are more accurate and helpful.

Typically, this restructuring begins during therapy sessions and is continued through the use of homework assignments in which the client is expected to use this more adaptive "self-talk" in real-life situations. It can be, of course, quite challenging for clients to actually apply this new information at the "point of performance"--the times and places in their lives where they typically engage in self-defeating thoughts.

In assigning therapeutic homework to child clients, it is important to remember that children may need varying degrees of "scaffolding" at the point of performance in order to successfully carry out such assignments. Enlisting the help of the child's caregivers is often the most vital type of scaffolding. However, additional scaffolding can be put in place through the use of "mediators"--tools that serve to remind the child of the knowledge gained in the therapy session.

Application/Treatment Modality:

Home assignment

Goal:

With this activity the child:

  • identifies an upcoming stressful or challenging situation.

  • formulates short, positive statements that can use replace automatic anxious, angry and/or upsetting thoughts.

  • creates postcards to provide additional scaffolding at the upcoming "point of performance."

Materials:

Encouraging Words postcards (Pages 51-52)

1. Talk to the child about the upcoming event.

2. Review some of the automatic, unhelpful thoughts and behaviors that they want to change. Help them to formulate statements that will be helpful and encouraging.

> *Let's think of some things that you can say to yourself when (X happens) that will help you to feel calm. We'll write them on this card, and you can take it home with you. That way, when (X happens) you can pull out the card and know just what to say to yourself.*

3. Help the child to think of statements that are specific to that particular situation, reassuring and realistic. Have the child put the statements in his or her own words.

4. One way for the child to use the Encouraging Words card is prior to the event, as a sort of rehearsal. For example, if the child is anxious about a performance, they could read the card on the way to the performance. If the child gets upset easily at birthday parties, they can review the encouraging words with a parent prior to leaving for the party.

5. It might also be helpful for the child to practice the self-calming techniques at the same time, using the *Cool-Down Rating Scale* to self-monitor. (Page 56)

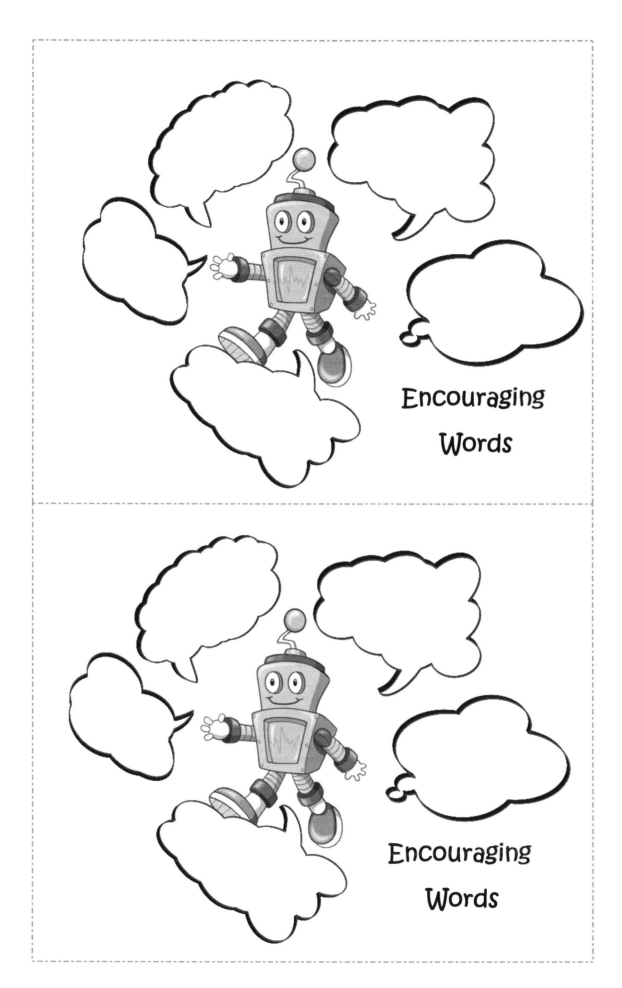

SLOW DOWN and GET CALM

Rationale:
Children may have difficulty calming themselves down after becoming emotionally upset. This activity helps children to understand and pay close attention to bodily reactions to upsetting events and to learn strategies for self-calming.

Treatment Modality: Individual, Family, Group (ages 4 to 12)

Goal:
In this activity children:
- learn that self-calming is a skill that can be practiced and improved.
- practice concrete strategies to slow and deepen their breathing and relax their muscles.
- use a tool for self-monitoring *The Cool-Down Rating Scale*.

Materials:
1. Slow Down and Get Calm picture (Page 55)
2. A bottle of bubbles and/or a small pinwheel (available from party supply retailers)
3. The *Get Calm Rating Scale* (Page 56)
4. A digital timer (or a watch or clock with a second hand)

This activity has two parts:
1) an INTRODUCTORY PLAY ACTIVITY to be carried out in the therapist's office.
2) an ASSIGNMENT to be demonstrated in the office and carried out at home.

Part 1: INTRODUCTORY PLAY ACTIVITY

1. Begin this activity by telling the child:

   *We are going to play a game called Get Calm. In this game, we **shift** from being upset to being cool and calm. Everyone gets upset from time to time. Even animals get upset. And when we get upset, our bodies react. Think of a cat when it sees a big barking dog. First, the cat's brain sends an alarm: **Something is wrong!** When its body gets that **alarm**, the cat*
   1) arches its back and 2) extends its claws and 3) hisses.

2. Demonstrate all three behaviors. (You can also show the picture of the upset cat on page 35). Then tell the child:
   *Pretend you are a cat and your brain has sent an alarm that **Something is wrong!** Show me how your body reacts.*
   Encourage the child to act out the cat's response. Allow the child to have fun with this.

3. Then tell the child:

   *You did a great job of showing how a cat reacts when its brain sends the message that something is wrong. That's a **good thing** when there is a danger, like when a mean dog might want to hurt the cat. Then the cat's body is ready to **do something!** -- to either fight the dog or to run away fast.*

   But what if the dog turns out to be a nice dog that just likes to hear itself bark and wouldn't hurt a flea?

   *Then the cat doesn't want to stay all upset. As soon as a cat knows that it is safe, it slows down. It switches from a **Something is wrong!** cat to a **cool and calm** cat. A **something is wrong!** cat is ready to fight or run. A **cool and calm** cat is ready to play with a toy or to curl up for a cat nap.*

   To slow down and get calm, the cat
   1) stretches its body
   2) relaxes its muscles, and
   3) yawns and takes a deep breath.
   It stops thinking about the dog and thinks about something else instead.

4. Demonstrate all three behaviors. Then tell the child:
   *Let's practice switching from a **something is wrong!** cat to a **cool and calm** cat.*
   *When I say **Something is wrong!** that's our cue to pretend to see a barking dog.*
   *But when I say **slow and calm**, that's our cue to take a deep breath, relax and be ready to play or rest.*

5. Practice switching from upset to calm. You may want to let the child take a turn giving the cues.

(Continued on next page)

After completing the play activity, tell the child:

*Your assignment is to practice at home so that you can get really, really good at making the switch from upset to calm. To do that you need to pay close attention to two things: **1st**, your breath and **2nd**, your muscles. I'm going to show you a special way to **breathe deeply** and a special way to **relax the muscles in your body**.*

DEEP BREATHING

1st, *let's practice breathing. We'll use these bubbles to help us. We will each take a **deeeep** breath and then let it out **slooooowly**. When we breathe out, let's see if we can make a big bubble and not burst it.*

Alterative #1 - Use a pinwheel instead of bubbles:

When we breathe out, let's see how long we can keep the pinwheel moving. The deeper and slower we breathe, the longer we'll be able to keep the pinwheel going.

Alterative #2 - Use a "pretend candle" instead of bubbles:

Put your finger in front of your mouth and pretend it's a candle. Pretend that there is a flame and when we breathe out, we want to make the flame move and flicker, but we don't want to blow it out. So we have to let our breath out very slowly and gently.

Practice this several times. If desired, make it more challenging by timing the length the out-breath, using a digital timer or a watch with a second hand. Once the child has shown some success at deep breathing, move on to the next step (which also involves deep exhalation of breath):

MUSCLE RELAXATION

Now, *let's learn to relax our bodies by stretching and then releasing our muscles. We are going to make "Air Angels.*

How to make an "Air Angel"

- Put your hands (palms together) in front of you stomach.
- Slowly, raise your hands straight above your head (your ears will be between your arms).
- Standing on tip-toes, stretch your whole body up as tall as you can.
- Hold that tight, tight. Make your muscles **very tense**.
- Now let's try to stretch and tighten up a little bit more. Stay like that and hold your breath.
- Now, **slooooowly** lower your arms to your sides, like fluffy angel's wings.
- As you slowly bring down your arms and let your hands fall to your side, breathe slowly out, and let your muscles switch from **tense** to **relaxed**.
- Pay attention and notice how it feels as you let your whole body relax and get calm down.

Practice this several times. Make sure that the child really feels the difference between the **tension** with arms and body outstretched and the **release** of muscles as they breathe out and relax their arms and body.

SELF-MONITORING

After doing this a time or two, introduce the concept of *self-monitoring,* using the *Get Calm Rating Scale* (Page 50). The purpose of the rating scale is to evaluate the degree of relaxation that you feel as you breathe deeply and relax. Show the child the rating scale and model how to use it. Initially, do not use a rating of "1" (the most relaxed) when you evaluate yourself; model improving your performance.

Next, give the child the rating scale and have the child demonstrate. Make adjustments or give suggestions as needed.

Finally give the child their own copy of the rating scale (and a pinwheel and/or bubbles if available) and tell the child:

Practice your deep breathing and muscle relaxation at home. Use the Cool Slow Down rating scale to check how well you are doing. Next time we'll practice together again.

Suggestions for carrying out assignment: It will be helpful to have the assistance of the child's parent in practicing these self-calming strategies at home. Initially, this should not be done in stressful situations (when the child is already upset). Instead, begin by practicing at a neutral time such as bedtime. This allows the child to gain confidence and lays a foundation for the child to later use the same strategies under more stressful circumstances.

The therapist may want to provide a chart for the child to record practice sessions (and also consider providing some sort of reward for completing the chart). When stressful circumstances arise, the child may need a reminder (or cue) to use the strategies that he or she has learned. But the more often the strategies have been practiced at neutral times, the easier it will be to implement them under stressful situations.

Slow Down and Get Calm

SLOW DOWN

55

Get Calm Rating Scale

How to make rating scales:
1) Print on heavy paper.
2) Cut on outer lines to make three rating scales.

Golden Path Games 2016

WHAT'S THE PROBLEM, WHAT'S THE PLAN?

Rationale:

Cognitive-behavioral therapy focuses on both cognitive and behavioral flexibility. Problem-solving is therefore often an important component in CBT and is typically incorporated by teaching a structured, step-by-step strategy. *What's the Problem? - What's the Plan?* presents the problem-solving process in a graphic, step-by-step method that will be easy for children to grasp. Based on proven strategies, the five-part structure gets family members actively involved in discussing a problem and agreeing on a solution.

Application/Treatment modality: Family therapy (can be adapted for individual therapy)

Goals:

In this activity family members:

- select an issue the family is struggling with and discuss the problem.
- brainstorm for ideas to solve the problem.
- evaluate those ideas and choose the best solution.
- make a plan for implementing the chosen solution.
- make a commitment to evaluate the outcome of the plan at a later date.

Materials Needed:

1. **What's The Problem?** (Page 58) and **What's the Plan?** (Page 59)
2. What's My Plan? (for individual therapy) (Page 60)

Begin with a problem that the family has presented in therapy.

1. The family members present jointly define the problem: The more specifically the problem can be defined, the more successful the solutions are likely to be. For example, rather than defining the problem as "School mornings are horrible" have the family be specific about what makes them horrible: "Jack does not get out of bed on time" or "There are too many things to do in the morning and we get angry with one another." Write the problem in the section provided at the top of the *What's The Problem?* Worksheet.

1. Next, each person reflects on the problem from their perspective. Using the table at the bottom worksheet, complete each column, one at a time. First, list the family members present. Then each person tells what they do (or fail to do) that contributes to the problem. Next, each person tells how much stress the problem causes for them.. Finally, each person tells how they think their family life will benefit if the problem is solved.

2. Using the *What's the Plan?* Worksheet, the family brainstorms for ideas that may help to solve the problem, following the brainstorming guidelines on the worksheet. The therapist may need to keep them focused on generating ideas by stepping in if they begin to evaluate ideas before the process is complete. Even if they say they can't think of ten ideas, have them persist and fill in all of the rows.

   Note: The parents may need to include ideas about what consequences will follow for compliance or lack of compliance with the plan.

3. After they evaluate the ideas, have them choose one to implement. It's OK to combine a couple of ideas to create a plan, but don't allow them to select too many ideas as they that may make it less likely that they will follow through.

4. Have each person state clearly what their role will be in implementing the plan they have created and write that down in the "Our plan" section.

5. Finally, have the family decide on a time to evaluate their plan. Let them know that their plan may not work perfectly and that's OK; the important thing is that they have made a plan together. They can learn a lot by trying it out, seeing what is working and what is not and making changes. Express confidence that there is a solution to the problem and they have the means to find the solution by working together.

Variation: For individual therapy, follow the same procedure, but use the simplified worksheet (Page 54)

What's the Problem?

Think carefully about the problem and describe what it looks like in your family's life:

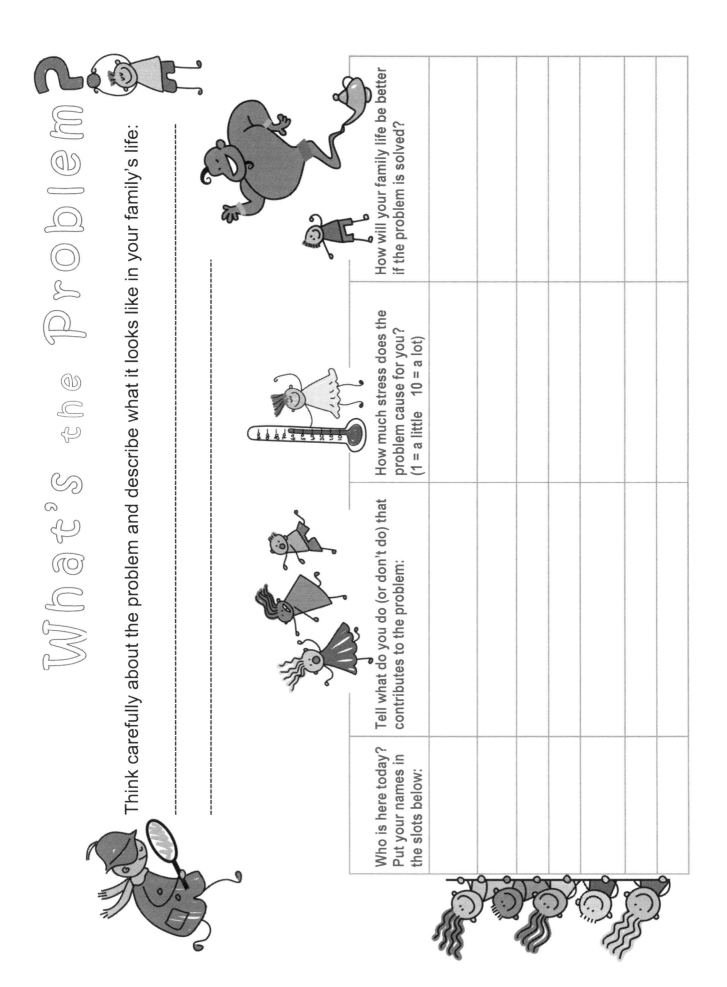

Who is here today? Put your names in the slots below:	Tell what do you do (or don't do) that contributes to the problem:	How much stress does the problem cause for you? (1 = a little 10 = a lot)	How will your family life be better if the problem is solved?

What's the Plan?

How To Brainstorm:

1) THINK OF IDEAS: Write one idea in each row, next to a puzzle piece. Write ALL ideas that come to mind. Don't evaluate yet. Even ideas that seem silly at first are welcome during brainstorming, because sometimes a silly idea will lead the way to a great idea!

2) DISCUSS IDEAS: After you have filled in all of the rows, talk about each idea. You can also use the next column to rate the ideas, from 1 to 10, according to how much each idea will help the problem.

3) CHOOSE IDEAS: Make a plan: Decide which idea (or combination of ideas) will best help the problem. Put a star in the last column next to those ideas. The stars show your plan! Now fill out the box below.

OUR PLAN

Name		Tell what each of you will do to put the plan into action.

Decide on a time and place to meet again, see how your plan is working, and make changes if needed.
Date: Time:
Place:

BRAINSTORM for ideas to help solve the problem:

What's My Plan?

1. What's The Problem?

 2. BRAINSTORM *for ideas*
   to help solve the problem:

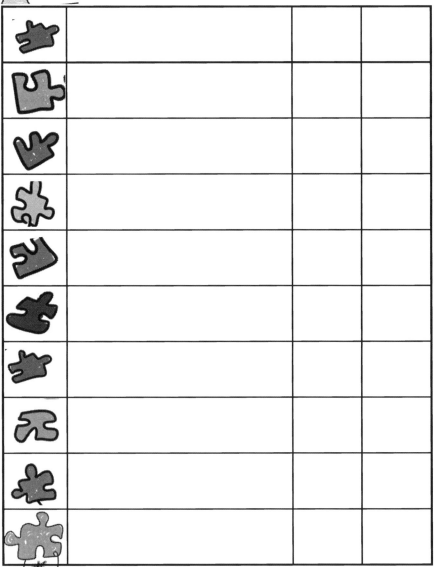

How To Brainstorm:

a) THINK OF IDEAS: Write one idea in each row, next to a puzzle piece. Write ALL ideas that come to mind. Don't evaluate yet. Even ideas that seem silly at first are welcome during brainstorming, because sometimes a silly idea will lead the way to a great idea!

b) DISCUSS IDEAS: After you have filled in all of the rows, talk about each idea. You can use the 2nd column to rate the ideas, from 1 to 10, according to how much each idea will help the problem.

c) CHOOSE IDEAS: Make a plan: Decide which idea (or combination of ideas) will best help the problem. Put a star in the last column next to those ideas.

The stars show your plan! Now fill out the box below:

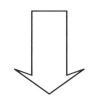

3. Here's my plan: (**What** are you going to do? Tell **where** and **when** you'll do it. **Who** will help you?)

Decide on a time to evaluate your plan, see how it's working, and make changes if needed.
Date: Time: Place:

STAY ON TRACK MAP

Rationale:

Even if a family comes up with a good plan for solving a problem, children who have difficulty regulating their emotions and behavior may not be able to reliably follow through with their part of the plan. When "in the moment", they may be overwhelmed and fail to inhibit the type of unhelpful responses that they identified in the *Don't Do It!* Activity. If they fail to inhibit, or interrupt, those responses, they will have difficulty focusing on the the alternative thoughts and ideas that they identified in the *Are You a Careful Thinker?* and the *What's the Plan?* Activities.

This does not mean that the child does not *want* to do their part; they may just need additional support at the "point of performance" -the time and place where they must muster their resources and remember to use the CBT strategies that they have learned in therapy.

Application/Treatment modality: Individual and family therapy

Goals:

With this activity, the child:

- confirms their intention to follow a plan.
- identifies the unhelpful behaviors they need to stop.
- identifies the actions and thoughts that will help them to stay on track with the plan.
- has the option of asking the parent to provide a cue if they start to get off track with the plan.

Materials Needed:

Stay On Track Map (Pages 62-63)

1. Tell the child:

   You and (your family) have made a good plan. Now the next step is stay on track and follow the plan. Sometimes it can be hard to stick with a plan, because we get distracted with other things; then we get off-track. So, today we are going to make a map that will help you stay on track with your plan, and help you know when you are getting off-track so you can say "Don't Do It! and stop yourself.

2. Give the child a copy of the map.

   The green light is by this big path. When you are on that path, you are "on track" to follow the plan. So, on the path, let's write some of the things you need to do to follow the plan.

3. Have the child name things that they need to do to be on track. If desired, you can also include things that the child can say to himself or herself.

   *The paths with the red light are paths that take you off-track. We don't want to get off-track when we are following a plan, so let's think about the things that you might need to **stop** yourself from doing. So, we'll write some things that you have to remember **not** to do on those paths.*

4. The map on page 63 has the *Don't Do It* guy in the corner of the map. This can be used if the child wants to plan for reminders from the parent.

   Remember when we played Red Light, Green Light and you had to stop something you had already started to do? Just in case you forget and start to get off-track let's come up with a cue that (your parent) can give you. Maybe the cue could be the words Red Light like we did in the game, or maybe you can think of another cue.

   Write the cue in the speech bubble.

5. Finally, help the child make a plan to have the map available at the "point of performance."

   *You've got a **great** map here to remind you what to do and what not to do. Now where will you put it and when will you look at it?*

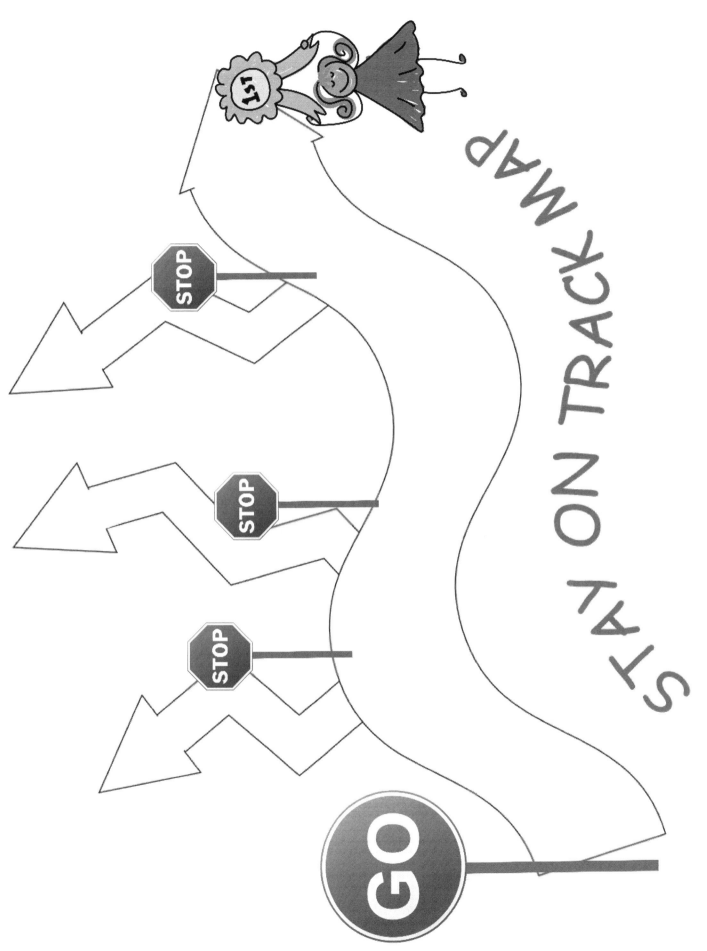

STAY ON TRACK MAP

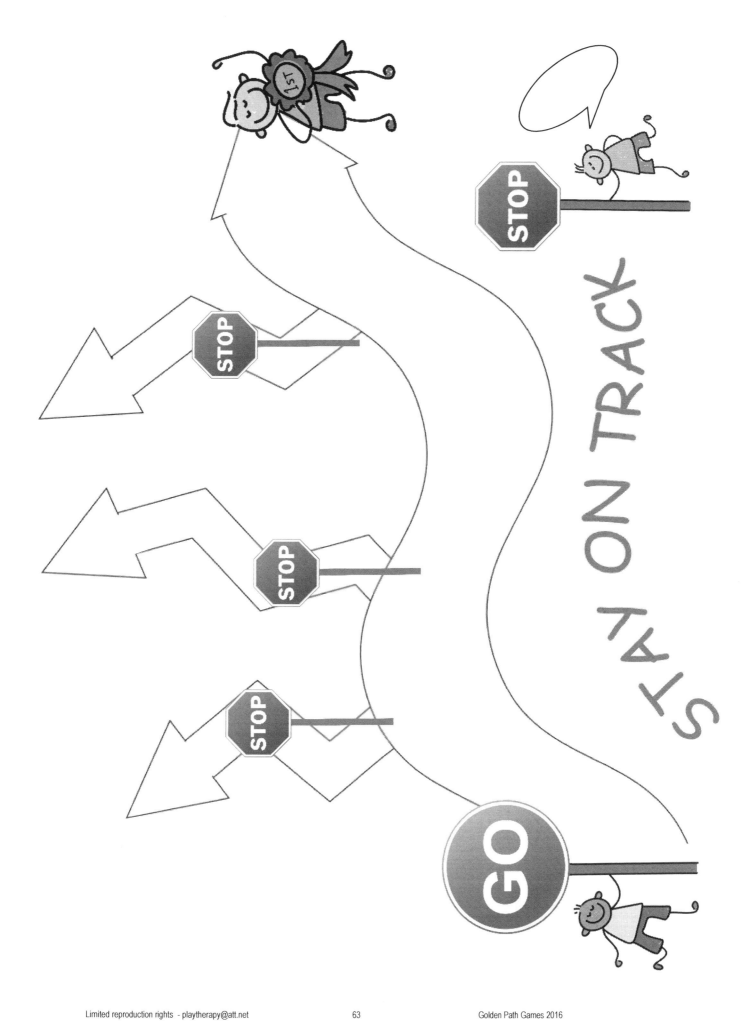

63

for purchasing this print edition of **Let's THINK About Feelings**.

As an owner of the paperback edition,
you are entitled to 50% off your purchase
of the **full-color digital** edition.

With the digital edition,
you can save the pages to your computer
and **print full-color activities** as you need them.

Find more CBT resources including the digital edition at
www.playtherapyworks.com

Use code: **PRINT**

to save 50% on the digital edition of **Let's THINK About Feelings**.
THIS DISCOUNT IS **NOT TRANSFERABLE**
AND IS FOR THE **ONE-TIME USE** OF CUSTOMERS
WHO HAVE PURCHASED **Let's THINK About Feelings** AS A PAPERBACK BOOK.

For comments, questions, suggestion, requests, contact us at
playtherapy@att.net

Cartoon people drawings by Prawny

Made in the USA
San Bernardino, CA
26 September 2016